How to Enrich Your Retirement

*How to Make Your Money Work
Smarter and Harder*

John T. Cross

*Principal partner of leading wealth management group, St. James
Place, and member of Million Dollar Round Table and Top of the Table*

iUniverse, Inc.
New York   Bloomington

How to Enrich Your Retirement
How to Make Your Money Work Smarter and Harder

iUniverse books may be ordered through booksellers or by contacting:

iUniverse
1663 Liberty Drive
Bloomington, IN 47403
www.iuniverse.com
1-800-Authors (1-800-288-4677)

Because of the dynamic nature of the Internet, any Web addresses or links contained in this book may have changed since publication and may no longer be valid. The views expressed in this work are solely those of the author and do not necessarily reflect the views of the publisher, and the publisher hereby disclaims any responsibility for them.

ISBN: 978-0-595-44933-0 (sc)
ISBN: 978-0-595-69389-4 (dj)
ISBN: 978-0-595-89255-6 (e-book)

Printed in the United States of America

iUniverse rev. date: 6/15/2009

To my darling wife, Sherry, who has always supported me in everything I have done and always inspired me to achieve great things

Contents

Foreword

Before I met John Cross, I thought I knew a thing or two about investments. However, as a fortysomething professional woman, I knew nothing about inheritance tax. Why would I? I had plenty of time to think about that. After spending an hour or two with John, I changed my mind on both counts.

John has a unique way of making these complex rules and regulations easy to understand. He calls this way 'unbundling' and he draws on his extensive client successes to illustrate his points. 'You can't price a memory' was wisdom I'd never heard from a financial consultant before, but John made me rethink my approach to my money. The financial sector is full of jargon, and the papers and journals are filled with dos and don'ts. It was refreshing to hear John break it down into several steps. Those steps now form the basis of this book you have in your hands.

I had approached John about writing a book. I had heard through a mutual friend that he had a unique way of helping people invest and save inheritance tax. From reading the bookstore shelves, I knew this was sorely needed. Someone needed to debunk a lot of the theory and make this process easy to understand. And that is what John has achieved in his book. John's engaging and professional approach has made him the most successful principal partner in St. James Place, and I think he will reach a new audience with this publication.

Amanda Seyderhelm, 2008

http://www.successfulwomenblog.com

Acknowledgements

I would like to thank Dan Sullivan and Strategic Coach Inc. of Toronto for the motivation and inspiration to write this book over the last ten years. My good friend, Tony Ward, encouraged me enormously. Amanda Seyderhelm provided her help and ideas in putting this book together. And Chris Coote, my son-in-law who works with me at the Royston office and has worked with me on many of the ideas in this book. Finally, Sue Porter has spent many hours labouring over the drafts and redrafts of this book.

About the Author

I have written this book based on my thirty-five years of experience in the financial services industry and over thirty years of experience of specialising in investment planning and inheritance tax planning.

You often hear the following phrase used in a derogatory way, 'Trust me. I'm a financial adviser.' But I use it all the time. Why? In the end, you do have to find a financial adviser who you can trust and a company who you feel comfortable working with.

You will no doubt respond, 'That's easier said than done, especially with the pension and endowment mis-selling scandals that have gone on over the last ten years in the UK and especially when you see companies like Equitable Life, one of Great Britain's biggest life companies, get into financial difficulties.'

However, I always tell my clients to follow their gut reaction. If you feel comfortable in dealing with me and feel you can trust me, then I am the financial adviser to look after your affairs. I always say that I could not have done what I have done over the last thirty-five years, had it not been based on the highest ethical and moral principals, you just have to trust me on this.

If you would like to receive a copy of my free DVD, please log on to my Web site at www.sjpp.co.uk/johncross. You will also find all of the seminars listed on this web site, along with registration information. Alternatively, please telephone our Royston Office on +44 (0)1763 247411.

Part One

Plan for Your Retirement

Chapter One

Introduction

This book is about how to enrich your retirement by making your money work smarter, harder, and longer for you. It will also show you how you might save large amounts of inheritance tax. The purpose of this book is to try and help those UK readers to unbundle their thinking and get down to basics so it is easy to make a decision about retirement planning.

In my experience as a financial adviser in the UK, I have observed that most clients find financial choices overwhelming. In particular, as they get older, they find it increasingly difficult to look after their finances as they invariably lose sight of what their financial objectives are. In effect, they become all 'bundled up' and find themselves totally unable to make a decision. The unbundling process, therefore, is designed to simplify the decision-making process in order to enable those reading this book to make decisions based on what their financial requirements really are.

This book is so important because you are likely to live much longer than you had anticipated you would when you were in your mid-forties or early fifties. This makes it paramount that you think medium- to long-term plans with regard to your investments. This is especially so when you retire. The old idea that it would all be over after seventy years no longer applies. According to the latest government statistics, the average life expectancy after retirement is at least twenty-three years.

In this book, I'm going to show you how to make your money work longer, smarter, and harder for you. I will show you how to make income king for your retirement and get your money to work for you rather than the Inland Revenue. Although this book is primarily designed for those living in the UK, the investment principles, as described later, are universal.

I believe it is crucial that many people, especially those who are retired, learn to change their mind-set. This is important because, otherwise, you would just keep accumulating your pot of gold and not spending your capital. When you were at work, you received your salary cheque each month, which was usually paid directly into your bank account. Now that you have retired, you will be receiving your pension, which, again, will be usually paid into your bank account. But, for 99 per cent of the people I meet, there is a considerable difference between the salary they were earning prior to their retirement and the pension they will receive on retirement. Even people who retire in the UK on a maximum pension of two-thirds final salary will still see a considerable drop in their income. However, many clients I meet have a pension income of less than half the income they were earning prior to retirement. This is especially so with widows who, on the death of their spouse, will often only receive half of their late spouse's pension.

Just because you have retired, doesn't mean you no longer have any expenses. In fact, all of your expenses will continue in your retirement just the same as they did prior to your retirement. The telephone bill won't suddenly reduce dramatically. You won't spend less on heating. In fact, you might spend more because you will be at home more. You will still continue to live in the world to which you have become accustomed over the preceding years.

To enrich your retirement, you need to change your mind-set and take the following steps:

1. Determine your basic retirement financial strategy.
2. Discuss plans and priorities with your partner (if you have one).
3. Stop accumulating; start spending.
4. Enjoy your money. You can't take it with you.
5. Think of your capital as a reservoir of money that will provide you with the necessary income.
6. Gear your investments to produce more income; income is king in retirement.
7. You will probably live longer than you thought.

Decide What Your Basic Retirement Strategy Is

My starting point is to suggest that, when you retire or are near this point, you need to sit down and think about your money. Then create an appropriate investment and inheritance tax strategy that will take you through the rest of your life in a tax-efficient manner, yet allow you to enjoy all of the things you always promised yourself you would. Here are some key questions you might ask yourself:

Key Questions

1. How and where do I want to live?
2. Is health care a major consideration right now? Will it be in the future?
3. Do I wish to provide for my children or grandchildren, or are there others I wish to provide for?

The questionnaires in the appendix will help you sort out your priorities. Once you've established your basic financial goals in retirement, it's time to work with your spouse, if you have one. Both of you should be on the same wave length about strategies and goals.

Discuss Plans/Priorities with Your Significant Other

I am astounded when I meet clients who do not talk to their significant others or spouse about money. It is the most important subject there is when you have retired. It is important that you both understand what the present position will be and what the future position will be, particularly if one of you dies. However, almost daily, I meet clients who do not share this information with others. This can sometimes cause a real problem.

I attended a meeting at a client's home recently. The husband was in quite a distressed state because he had had a major row with his spouse that morning.

When I asked him what the row had been about, he said he had told his wife that he had arranged a meeting with me, but he did not want her to be present. He admitted to me that he was very secretive about his financial affairs. He explained that he had been married for ten years, and although he loved his wife very much, he just felt he could not share his financial situation with her.

To use his words, he realised he was being 'stupid' and making a major error in not trusting his wife with his financial information. I suggested a further meeting be arranged with him and his wife so we could sit and discuss the financial situation jointly. I am pleased to say that he did see common sense, and a subsequent meeting was arranged. I would urge you to talk to your significant other about finances. Even though you talk to your significant other daily, how often do you talk about money? How often do you discuss your investments? How often do you examine your financial objectives, both short- and long-term goals?

Unfortunately, often by default, some women end up in this position of having to actively manage their money in their retirement. They didn't really mean it to happen that way. It sort of just happened. Forgive me, ladies, for a second while I refer to one or two of the male chauvinists reading this book. I know there's one or two. You chaps look after the portfolio. You don't get your significant other involved. You pop your clogs and expect her just to carry on in the same old way, looking after all the investments. For the last twenty-five years, you haven't been telling her what you've been investing in and why.

I always encourage married couples to come to my seminars together. Very often, when I meet them afterwards for one-on-one sessions, they tell me that they had gone years without talking to each other about finances, but they have now started to put that right. Sometimes, it's for the first time in their lives.

I now insist that all of my clients complete a document called 'What I Own and Where It's Kept.' Once they have completed this document, I then ask them to store it with their wills or other important documents. It is amazing how useful this proves to be. I realised the importance of this type of document when one of my clients died last year. His wife had no idea which solicitor had drawn up her late husband's will. The client lived in Bedford. His wife thought he had dealt with a solicitor somewhere in Bedfordshire, but she just wasn't sure. We eventually tracked down the solicitor who had organized her husband's will and affairs, but it took eleven telephone calls to eleven different solicitors.

It's appalling how many widows I meet who have no idea whatsoever as to what their late husband's financial position was and what the investments are.

A couple of years ago, during one of my seminars, a lady stood up and advised the other ladies in the room to make sure they had a joint bank account with their spouse before he died. She explained that her husband had died some time ago and his pension was paid into his bank account in his name. She couldn't get probate on the estate, and she hadn't been able to draw his pension. He should have had a joint bank account.

She could have asked her bank to pay this money into the joint account instead of his account. From there, she could have then drawn the pension. Little things like that can make a massive difference to your finances. It's really important to get this right so you can sit back and relax. You won't have to think or worry about your investments going forward.

Stop Accumulating and Start Spending

I don't mean you should stop acquiring more wealth as you grow older. However, there is no point in accumulating just for the sake of it just so the Chancellor of the Exchequer will get a larger slice of your estate when you die. I never cease to be amazed by how often I meet clients who just keep accumulating money purely for the sake of doing so without any logic or reason. Of course, you need to make sure you have enough to take care of yourself for the rest of your life, especially with nursing homes and long-term health care in mind.

Gear Your Investments to Produce More Income

I am always appalled when I meet clients who have substantial investments and then tell me that they need more income. Invariably, when I look at their position, I find that all their investments are geared to capital growth. Virtually none is geared to income. This just doesn't make sense at all, especially when you have retired. Until the day you do retire, you definitely need to aim for capital growth. But, on that one particular day, the rules change. You need your investments to produce more income to enable you to maintain your lifestyle going forward for the rest of your and your significant other's lives.

Once retired, income is king. Capital is merely an instrument for providing the level of income you need. It is very important that you look at your investments in terms of producing maximum income to supplement your pension and maintain the lifestyle that you wish to enjoy for the rest of your life.

If you do not have sufficient income, it is important to be brave and move your existing investments into income-producing investments to supplement your state and personal pensions. Previously, these investments may have, quite rightly, been geared for capital growth up to your sixty-fifth birthday. It is interesting how many clients I meet with substantial amounts of investments which are geared towards capital appreciation when they actually need more income. Always remember that income is king when you retire. Anything that impacts your income has an immediate impact on you. Anything that impacts the capital value of your investments does not.

In other words, if you could rearrange some of your investments so they produce an extra £5,000 of income per year, you would notice the effect immediately. However, if the value of your investment falls due to fluctuations in the stock market, the fact that your investment may be worth £5,000 less today than it was yesterday is irrelevant. It does not impact you at all because it is likely that the market will recover next week or next month. Your capital value will rise, and you won't have noticed the difference. With your income, however, you would notice the difference immediately.

You Will Probably Live Longer Than You Think

Why is this so important to you? Why I am banging the drum about this? I've got some very good news. It's the best news I'm going to give you in this book. Everyone reading this book, including myself, is going to live much longer than we thought we were. That's why you're going to have to make your money work longer, harder, and smarter for you. I'm a father and a grandfather, and I'm very proud of it. Both my parents, who are in their eighties, are still alive and doing very well. Both have outlived any actuarial assumption they would have made when they retired.

When my dad retired, at sixty-five, he thought he only had a few years to go. Some twenty years later, he, along with my mum, are still going like a steam train. Many of us are going to be in that position.

The Short-term Facts

If you are a sixty-five-year-old male married to a sixty-year-old female and both of you are retiring, one or both of you are going to live a minimum of twenty-three years according to the latest government statistics. That is the average life expectancy from retirement today. Only a hundred years ago, you were lucky if you got to be sixty or sixty-five. According to the latest government statistics, gentlemen aged seventy-seven years old just had their life expectancy increased by seven years. They'll likely live to at least eighty-five. For eighty-three-year-old ladies, they'll likely live to be at least ninety-five. It's staggering. One way or another, both my parents are likely to live at least another ten years.

The Cost of Long-term Nursing Care

About 20 per cent of you reading this book will require some form of long-term health and nursing care. So you've got to get your money to work harder because you may need that money to take care of you in a nursing home. It's amazing how many clients I met ten, fifteen, or twenty years ago who have now gone into a nursing home. Essentially, you have to make your money work for you harder and longer than ever.

Chapter Two

Enjoy Life! Spend Some of Your Money!

When I say start spending, I don't mean you should throw your money away. You should enjoy your retirement and do all of those things that you promised your spouse you'd do after you retired. Think about all those trips you planned and all those places you wanted to see. All of us have a lease on life, but none of us know how long it will last. So why not take your money and enjoy it while you can? I meet so many clients who tell me they had planned to do so much when they retired, but, somehow, they never quite got round to it. Then they found it was a day too late. They look back on their lives with bitterness and regret. I don't want anyone who reads this book to be in that position.

One of my clients is worth over £10 million. He has a seven-figure income from property development that he has made over the years. He and his wife don't have any children. However, when I visited him recently, his wife was at home. During a short break, she explained to me that she'd very much like to have a new Cartier watch for her birthday, which was going to cost a couple of thousand pounds. But her husband wouldn't buy her one because he said they couldn't afford it! What is the point in being worth £10 million if you can't buy your wife a nice watch for her birthday or wedding anniversary?

In a similar vein, one of my gentleman clients is in his nineties and is a multimillionaire. He still travels fairly extensively, but he'll only travel economy class on long flights. He refuses to upgrade to club or first class. He says it is just too expensive. Then he admits that he stopped enjoying the flying because it was so uncomfortable at the back of the plane. What possible logic is there in being a multimillionaire if you insist on travelling long trips at the back of the plane? In my view, you might as well not have the money. If you are in this position, you are certainly not enjoying it. So why don't you give it away to someone else who will enjoy it on your behalf?

You Can't Take It with You

Of course, if you could take it with you, it would be great. But we all know that you can't. But many of my clients act as if they actually can.

Jokingly, I ask my clients what they are planning to spend this money on when they get to the other side. They look at me with a mixture of amusement and embarrassment, as they admit that they won't be able to spend it on anything.

Example

At my seminars, I tell the story of a lady whose husband knew he had reached the end of his life, so he asked her to make him a solemn promise.

'What is it?' she asked.

He said, 'Look, we have been married for fifty years. Make the solemn promise first. Then I will tell you what I want you to do when I die.'

She agreed and made the promise.

She was surprised when he said, 'When I go, I want to take all of my money with me.' She told her best friend about this. They discussed what she should do. Shortly afterwards, her husband died. On the day of the funeral, her friend noticed the new widow went up to the coffin. With great ceremony, she placed a small box inside it before it was finally sealed.

After the internment, her friend rushed up to her and said, 'Oh, my dear, you didn't carry out the promise you had made to him, did you?'

'Yes,' said the new widow. 'I had made a solemn promise. After he died, I cashed in all of his investments, turned them into cash, and paid them into my bank account. What you saw me doing earlier today was putting a cheque into his coffin for the total amount. If he can cash it in and spend it when he gets to the other side, he is very welcome to it!'

This leads me back full circle to the previous nine points that I have just raised. It is no good acting as if you can take it with you because you and I know that you simply can't!

Think of Your Capital as a Reservoir

Think of your investments as a reservoir of money from which the income and capital may be withdrawn to provide the standard of living that you require. As long as the reservoir is growing, you are not living off your capital. Often, there is a distinct tax advantage in this strategy. You are taking withdrawals from your growing capital, which will only be subject potentially to capital gains tax. With the improvements in this tax as set out in the Finance Acts of 1982 and the Chancellor's budget statement in October 2007 and March 2008, it is likely that you will not exceed the exemptions. Your extra income provided by these withdrawals will therefore be tax-free.

I have a client of many years standing who always refused to take advantage of the capital gains tax allowances because he wouldn't pay the stockbroker's commission each year when he sold his shares. When the capital gains tax allowance was £6,000, the cost of exercising the sale would have been £200 in stockbroker's commission. No matter how hard I tried, he would never take advantage of stripping out the capital gain in order to spend it as income. Some years later, due to a family emergency, he had to cash in all of his shares. He paid a huge capital gains tax bill and suddenly realised that, if he had taken advantage of the annual allowance for the past ten years, he could have received £60,000 of tax-free capital. Instead, on the £60,000 capital gain, he paid £24,000 in tax compared with the £2,000 he would have paid in stockbroker's charges.

You Cannot Price a Memory

Of all the things we have access to during our lifetimes, memories are the most precious. I still look back and remember my grandparents. I was fortunate to have both my mother's parents and my father's parents alive until quite some time after I was married. I have such fond memories of them, especially my mother's father, who used to tell me and my brothers the most wonderful stories about what happened to him during the First World War and how he was shot three times. He used to keep us enthralled for hours with his stories. The memories I have of him are simply priceless.

Yet my grandfather never had any money. He was just an ordinary working man. He had no aspirations with regard to investments. All of his life, he lived in rented accommodations. He never owned a house nor any shares. He never had any other investments, which was typical of many people of his generation. Today, most people own their own homes. Even if they don't, they hope to do so one day. A large number of people own their own investment portfolio or have funds directly invested in equities through their pension funds. Maybe my grandfather didn't need to be investment-savvy, but that certainly isn't the situation today.

I would hope that your memories should be as precious. I do find it such a shame when clients want to do things and go places, but they won't because it is too expensive. What does the cost matter if it gives you a memory you carry with you for the rest of your life? Every year, I go skiing with my children and grandchildren. It has been my privilege to pay for this, and I don't care what it costs because I have such wonderful memories of seeing my grandchildren ski for the first time. We have such quality time together when we are skiing up in the mountains. You might say, quality time together is easy when you can afford it. But it doesn't have to be an expensive memory.

I have been with my grandchildren to see some of the Harry Potter movies, but I meet grandparents who would never dream of taking their grandchildren to the cinema nor out for a meal because it is too expensive. I have clients who won't take their wives out on their wedding anniversaries because it is too expensive. They miss so much as a result of their small-mindedness.

Chris Coote, who has been working with me for the past fifteen years, mentioned during a seminar introduction that I had recently celebrated my forty-third wedding anniversary. A lady came up to me in the coffee break and told me that she was celebrating her wedding anniversary that day. I congratulated her. She looked at me with a wry smile as she told me that, a month ago, her husband asked her if she would like to go out for lunch on their wedding anniversary. She accepted. What she didn't realise was that she had to come to one of my seminars first, and the lunch she would be getting for her wedding anniversary was a free one that I provided!

Memories are the most precious of all things. You just cannot price them, so stop counting the pennies. Enjoy your time in retirement.

You've spent the last sixty years scrimping, saving, and building your pot of gold. Now's the time to spend some of it and enjoy it. Go on that cruise you've always promised yourself. My wedding anniversary just passed. I've been married to my lovely wife, Sherry, for forty-three years. We went to Midsummer House in Cambridge, a beautiful restaurant. It's expensive, but it was very nice and a lovely experience. Now we're going on a cruise to Alaska. Both my wife and I have always wanted to take this cruise. We saw one advertised, so we booked it. I have a very big birthday coming up in twelve months. I have already booked another cruise to South America to visit countries I haven't seen before. I will also take the opportunity to go down to Antarctica, which is a place I have always wanted to visit. You can see, therefore, I am certainly spending some of my money. That's why I am encouraging you to spend some of yours.

I want you to enjoy some of your money. Go and find that long-lost brother you've always said you were going to find. Go on that trip to Australia you've always promised yourself. All those things you said you'd do, book them. Do it! In my sixty-five years of life on this planet, I've learnt something really important in life. You cannot price a memory. A memory costs whatever it costs.

I recently sat with a lady whose husband had just died. The lady was sobbing and telling me some of the stories about her life and the things they'd done. These were all priceless memories. You cannot put a price tag on them. I'm not saying you should throw money away. Remember, if you don't spend it and hold on to it, the government is going to have it anyway, as I will show you later.

I Told You So!

When I come to this point in my seminar, I see a couple, perhaps sitting at the back of the room, where one looks at the other and mumbles something along the lines of, 'This is what I am always saying to you.' Or I often see an elbow aimed at a partner. Then he or she looks at his or her partner and comments, 'I told you so!'

One lady told me how foolishly her husband was behaving with his money. He really did think he could take it with him. He wouldn't buy anything or go anywhere. Even worse, he wouldn't let her buy anything or go anywhere. The last few years of their life had been so frugal, and she was so miserable with it. She had told him that, when he died, she was going to blow a big chunk of it on a world cruise. Then she looked me straight in the eye and said, 'And, Mr Cross, you better believe I am.' If you have a life partner, you need to review your financial situation with this person. It's only fair and right to keep him or her informed about your monetary strategies.

Chapter Three

You've already started to look at your finances differently to achieve your objectives. When you retire, your situation has changed, so your financial needs are different. This chapter will give you a good overview of your investment options during retirement.

Making the Right Investment

Recently, a major financial group surveyed people in London and asked, 'Where's the best place to have been invested for the last four years?' Only 2 per cent of people said the stock market. In fact, that was the correct answer. The UK stock market has gone from thirty-two hundred points to sixty-five hundred points over that period, an increase of 103 per cent, which is well ahead of domestic property prices over the same period.

Investment Jungle

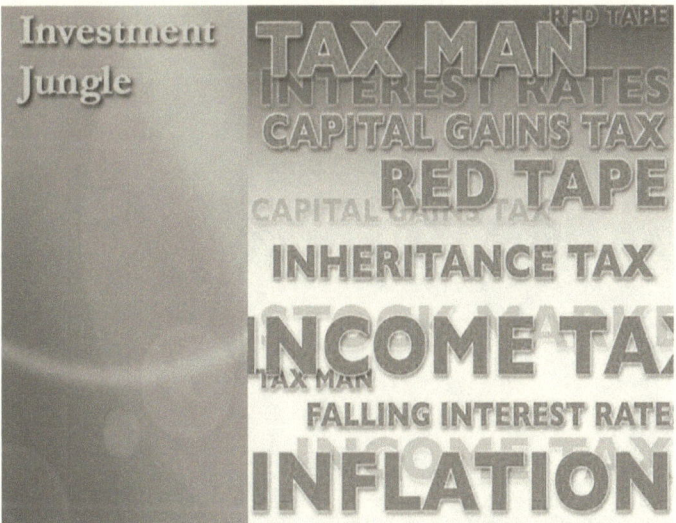

People tell me that it's a jungle out there. They question which are the right investments to make. There's income tax demands, the stock market, volatility, inflation/deflation, falling interest rates, rising capital gains tax, and inheritance tax.

But there isn't a best thing for you to be investing in right now. You need to look for a combination of those investments. You need to look at your investments in a different way. You need to look at your financial needs.

From my 35 years' experience these are the six most common needs that I find apply to most of my clients:-

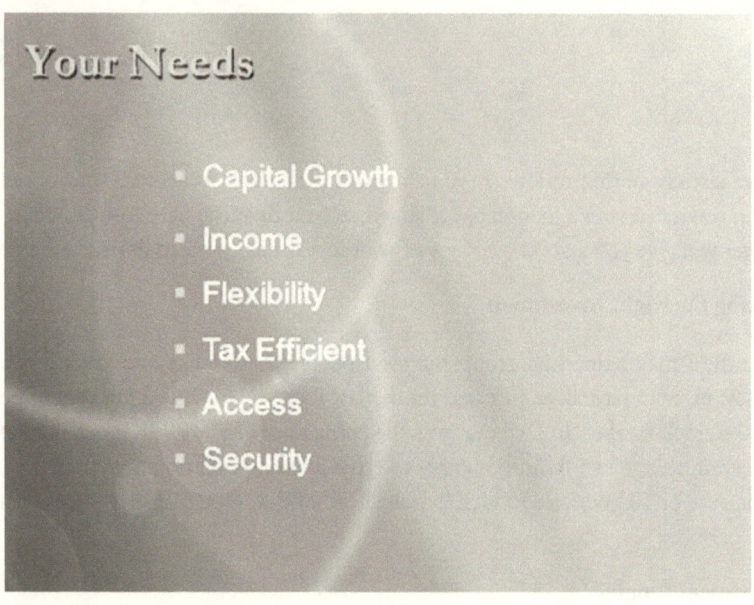

What Are You Aiming For

Fundamental Options

- Deposit
- Gilts
- Equities
- Property

What sort of things should you be investing in? Here are four areas of investments you should consider: property, gilts, deposits, and the stock market.

Property

Owning property (real estate) has been a wonderful investment for most people throughout their working lifetimes. It's probably the best investment you ever made. I am a Leicester boy, born and bred. When I left Leicester some thirty-five years ago to live in Hertfordshire, a four-bedroom, detached house in Hertfordshire cost £8,000. It seemed an awful lot of money at the time. My mortgage went up £5 a month, and I was wondering how I was going to pay the extra fiver. Not very long ago, my old house sold for about £400,000. I'm not still living there, but that's what it sold for. You and I both know that probably investing in property has been one of your best investments ever. Most of you reading this book know your property value has almost doubled or tripled in the last ten years.

I recently ran into some clients I hadn't seen in seven years. They told me their house was up for sale for £225,000. When I had spoken to them seven years ago, it was worth £85,000. So it had more than doubled over that period. Other clients told me that their house, which they had bought for £350,000 ten years ago, had just been sold for £850,000. All over the UK, it seems that clients are showing a substantial increase in the value of their property, though there has been a correction in the last twelve months. However, most people, even if we are facing a 30 per cent reduction in property prices as has been suggested, will still be showing a substantial profit on the property they bought five or ten years ago.

Domestic Property Doesn't Provide Income

When you retire, your property doesn't produce income for you because it's where you live. Now you could do what some of my clients have done in Cambridge and let a couple of bedrooms to students. That's fine. So you get some rental income from those students. Other than that, if it's your house, unless you sell the property and buy a smaller place or trade down and generate about £100,000 to do something with, you really can't generate income from your property. You could do an equity release scheme, which is basically like taking a lifetime mortgage. They're certainly worth considering in certain circumstances. So take a look. But take a very close look at them before you commit yourself. Make sure that it's right for you. If it is, you can take that money, invest it, and then generate income from it.

Property to Let Does Provide Income

If you have a commercial portfolio, for example, offices, warehouses, shopping precincts, and so on, this is property you can let. You could take that income and then get the capital appreciation as the investment increases over the years.

For most people, their property is the place where they live, and this does not produce income. So they're invested really in the other three areas. Let's look in more detail at these.

Gilts (Government Securities)

What exactly is gilt? Well, it's very simple really. Suppose the Prime Minister looks at his books and realises he is short of £100 he planned to use to widen the M1. He'd need to go to the Treasury Department and ask for more money. The Treasury would say he could have the money, and they would ask the Prime Minister two questions: What rate of interest shall we pay those members of the public who purchased this gilt? And for how long?

The Prime Minister might say that the going interest rate is about 5 per cent, so they'll offer that. They only need the money for one year because they've got lots of nice tax revenues coming in next year, so they'll be able to replace their funds then.

In very simple language, we have a 2009 treasury stock because it's going to mature in twelve months. It's at 5 per cent because that's the rate of interest the Treasury Department is going to pay. It's treasury stock because he's in the Treasury Department.

So if you got your financial paper every day, you could see the value of that stock on a day-to-day basis. And it would say, 'Treasury 5 per cent 2009.' You'd see the value because the value of it goes up and down all the time. You're guaranteed your £100 back in a year. You are guaranteed the 5 per cent gross, but you do have to pay tax on that. So the net return is about 4 per cent to a basic rate taxpayer. It's just over 3 per cent to a higher rate taxpayer. But the value of the money will go up and down.

Even though the value is guaranteed at maturity, the value of the investment will move up and down with market movements.

When the gilt matures in a year, you will get your money back. So, if you put £10,000 in the gilt five years ago and it's maturing today, you'd get your £10,000 back. It's absolutely guaranteed, and you would have got the interest, the 5 per cent, in the meantime. With those two guarantees, I suppose you've all got an awful lot of money invested in gilts? Probably not. Why? Gilts are a very technical subject, and you have to know what you're doing when you're buying and selling them. But a lot of you have gilts and didn't realise what they were called. In other words, they are national savings certificates. Now national savings certificates come in various guises. Some of the most popular are the capital bond, the ordinary national savings certificate, the guaranteed income bond, and the national savings income bond.

The Capital Bond (Now Renamed the Guaranteed Growth Bond)

John Major introduced the capital bond when he was Chancellor of the Exchequer which was before he became Prime Minister. When he introduced that some years ago, it was paying 11.5 per cent. Since then, interest rates have come down dramatically. As I write this book, the same capital bond is paying 4.5 per cent gross with a tax to pay on that. So the net return is approximately 3.5 per cent to a basic rate taxpayer and just below 3 per cent to a higher rate taxpayer.

The Ordinary National Savings Certificate

Now there's no tax to pay on the ordinary national savings certificate. I'm sure quite a few of you have got these. The national savings five-year certificate is currently paying 3.5 per cent net with no further tax. Seven years ago, the five-year national savings certificate was paying 8 per cent. So it has gone down from 8 per cent to 3.5 per cent. That's a massive drop. If you keep them, after the five years, you can go on to what's called the general extension rate. If you keep them over the five years, the current rate on national savings certificates that have matured is 3.15 per cent. So it's virtually 3 per cent. So, if inflation's 3.5 per cent and you're getting 3.15 per cent, you're really losing money, aren't you?

The problem with national savings certificates is that people tend to keep them too long. I've got a couple of good examples.

Example One

I have a national savings certificate for £1. It's actually viable. I could cash it in today. It was actually purchased at fifteen shillings and sixpence. A client sent it to me. It was taken out on November 11, 1918, or Armistice Day. So that one has been running for ninety years. Amazing, isn't it? Now, for a bit of fun, the gentleman who sent it to me rang up the National Savings Board to find out how much he would get back if he cashed it in. After ninety years of investing, he would have got back £5.11. Unbelievable, isn't it?

Example Two

People do keep national savings certificates for far too long. I had a case last year where clients called me and asked me to help them increase their mother's income because she was going into a nursing home. Out of the pile of stuff that they had left for me, the first thing I saw was a national savings certificate for £1,000. The lady had taken it out twenty-one years ago. Back then, £1,000 was a significant amount of money to invest. Today, after allowing for inflation, it's a comparatively small figure. So be aware of that. People do leave them there for too long.

The Pensioner Bond (Now Renamed the Guaranteed Income Bond)

The guaranteed income bond is the so-called granny and granddad's bond. You don't have to be a granny or a granddad in order to buy it. You just have to be over sixty now. The pensioner's bonds, as they're always referred to, are available as a five-year bond. At today's date, they are paying a 4.7 per cent gross, which is 3.5 per cent net to a basic rate taxpayer and 3 per cent to a higher rate taxpayer. The two-year bond is paying 4.85 per cent gross, which is 3.4 per cent to a basic rate taxpayer and 2.91 per cent to a higher rate taxpayer. the one-year bond is paying 4.95 per cent gross, which is 3.86 per cent to a basic rate taxpayer and 2.97 per cent to a higher rate taxpayer.

National Savings Income Bond

The monthly national savings income bond is quite popular with a lot of people. Again, ten years ago, that was paying 11.5 per cent. So, if you had invested £100,000 in a national savings income bond ten years ago, you would have received an income of £11,500. Unfortunately, that doesn't happen anymore. Today, the same person with the same investment is now getting 4.2 per cent gross. So his or her income has gone down from £11,500 to £4,200 gross.

Example Three

I saw a lady who'd got one of these national savings income bonds who had watched the income decrease and done nothing about it. With some of the investments I've shown her, she's getting a lot more income now. I'll show you these later. National savings income bonds are fine, but you shouldn't have too much money there. You also shouldn't leave it there for too long. For those of you with the maximum Premium Bonds at £30,000, do remember that your odds on winning the national lottery are now lower than your odds of winning the big one on the Premium Bond. The government has admitted that themselves!

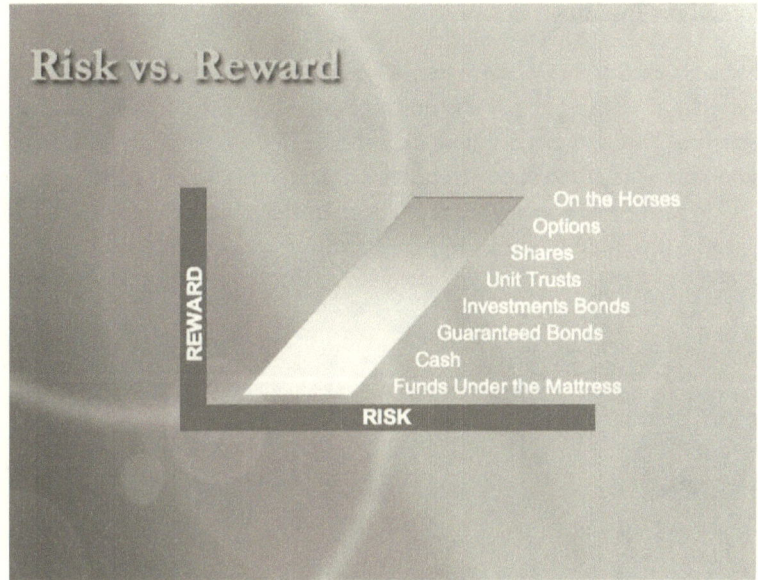

Risk versus Reward

The idea is that, the greater the risk, the greater the potential reward. By the same token, the greater the risk, the bigger the loss if it all goes wrong. Those of you who brought those high-tech Internet funds about eight years ago know that. But the key issue here is, 'Why don't you leave all the money in a tin box and keep it under the bed?'

If you leave it there and the house doesn't burn down, won't it always be there? Alternatively, why don't we go to the nearest racecourse and put it all on the 3.30 race? If it comes in at 3.31, you make a fortune. Of course, if it comes in at 4.31, you'll lose all your money!

People say, 'Don't be daft, John! I wouldn't keep it under the bed. Neither would I put it on the horses.'

I say, 'Well, I know you wouldn't. But where do you feel comfortable investing?'

It's amazing how people say, 'Well, somewhere between the two.'

I realise that, in order to get some sort of return, I have to be prepared to take a little bit of risk. So I have to ask, 'Why have so many people invested so much money in banks, building societies, and national savings and gilts?'

By the nature of the beast, they are a very low risk, so they are a very low reward investment. When you check the latest rates on the building societies and banks, some of you are in for a really nasty shock. You just might not realise how much they've come down.

Banks and the Building Society

Have you checked the very latest rates? If you compare them with those in 2007, to just see what the differences are, you might be rather surprised. If you looked at what happened in 2001 you can see how dramatically interest rates can fall. With the World on the edge of recession just imagine what the headlines might be if interest rates fall to 2% or less, as many are predicting. Imagine the impact this will have on your income, if your funds are on deposit.

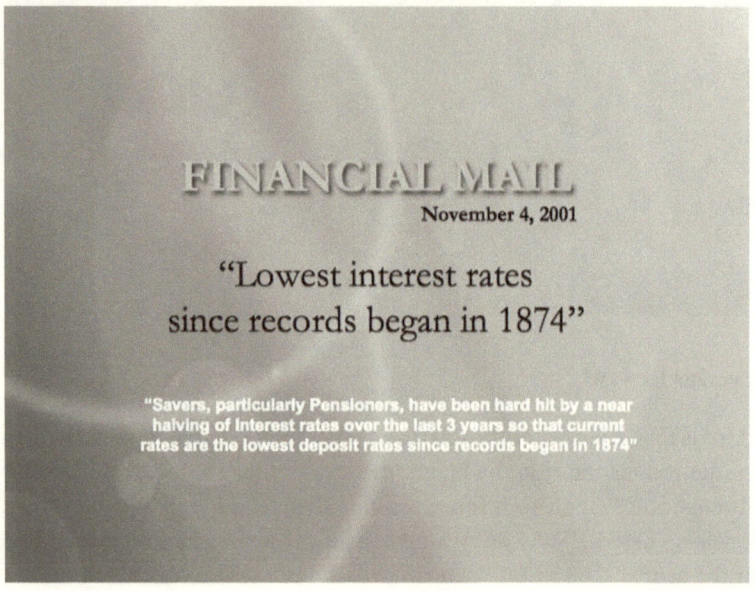

FINANCIAL MAIL

November 4, 2001

"Lowest interest rates
since records began in 1874"

"Savers, particularly Pensioners, have been hard hit by a near
halving of interest rates over the last 3 years so that current
rates are the lowest deposit rates since records began in 1874"

A *Financial Times* article on September 20, 2007 stated: "Against this backdrop, savers have been hit by the sharpest rate cuts in two years, with half of all banks and building societies cutting the savings rates by more than the recent Bank of England cut." Interestingly, money in a bank or building society does produce income and capital appreciation, but it goes to different people. You get the interest rate, that is, the low rate that the bank or building society will pay you right now. The person who makes the capital appreciation is the person who buys a property right now and sells it in five years for a handsome profit. Thank you very much! And it was your profit that they sold it for!

Example Four

I just had a wonderful example of that happening with one of my clients' daughters. She was due to be married, but she called off the wedding. Prior to the proposed marriage, she bought a house for £298,000. She and her fiancé had never actually moved in, but she moved in on her own. She had a £100,000 mortgage from a bank, and she put in the rest of the money from her previous property. After three years, she sold it for £398,000. She made £100,000 profit on the back of that mortgage that she had from the bank. That's what will happen in a few years. Somebody will borrow your money from the bank. He or she will buy a property down the road. Then he or she will sell it and make all the profit on it.

A Pound Equals a Pound

Why do people have all this money in banks, building societies, national savings certificates, gilts, and all the things I've talked about? Well, it's all summed up by the idea that a pound equals a pound. Did Hurricane Katrina impact the value of your pound? No, it didn't. Does terrorism impact the value of your money? No, it doesn't. It makes you feel uncomfortable and a bit insecure, but it doesn't impact the value of your money that's on deposit. That's why people leave it there. But you pay a terrible price for that. With inflation at a 3 per cent level and you're only getting less than 3 per cent net interest, you're not making any real money on your money. You're losing out!

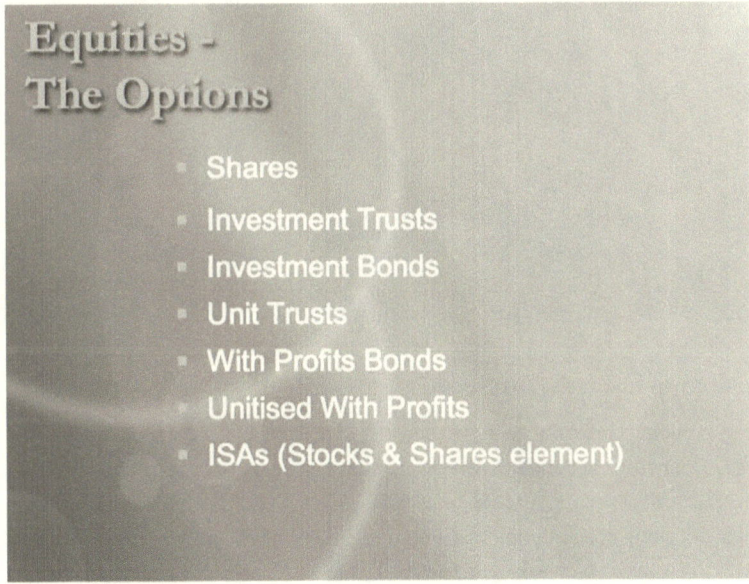

Equities –
The Options

- Shares
- Investment Trusts
- Investment Bonds
- Unit Trusts
- With Profits Bonds
- Unitised With Profits
- ISAs (Stocks & Shares element)

Equities: The Options

Where else should you invest it then? Shares? Trusts? Bonds? But here's the problem. If you give me £1,000 to invest in equities today, can you guarantee me that it will still be worth £1,000 the following day? The answer is that you cannot. But is it likely over the medium- to longer-term future that it will give me a good return on my money? The answer is that it will. In the last one, three, five, seven, ten, fifty, and three hundred and fifty years, you can only make two investments that will be guaranteed over a period to keep up with inflation. One is property; the other is stocks and shares.

Believe it or not, stocks and shares have always outperformed property over the medium- to longer-term basis. In the last five years, that's why the best place to be invested has been in stocks and shares. The FTSE Share Index has risen very strongly. Now it is showing a real return on clients' investments.

But people get worried about volatility because they look at markets on a short-term basis. You mustn't do this. You must always look at them on a medium- to long-term basis. Remember, you're going to live for the rest of your life in the future, however long that is. We hope that's a long time.

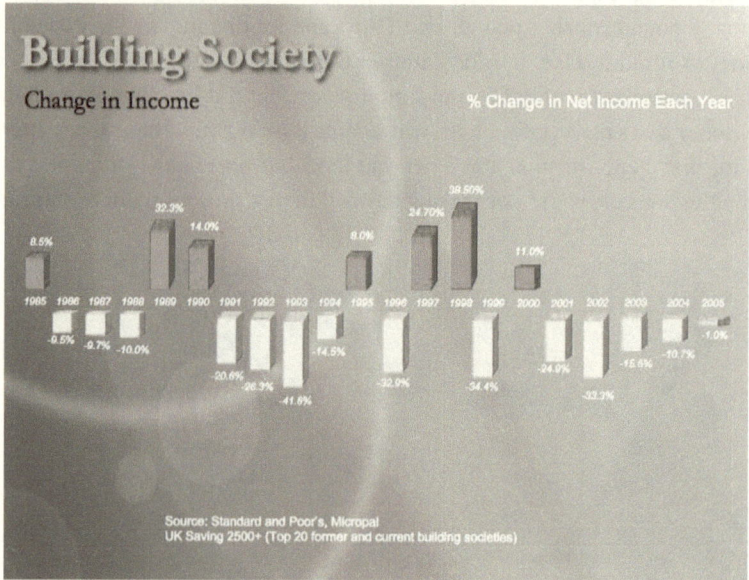

Up-and-down Income Is No Good

Look at bank and building society interest. Look at what's shown in the graph to see what's happened to the income one would expect to receive from those investments over the last twenty years. Interest rates have gone up and down many times. How can you plan your retirement finances if you don't know what you are going to actually be receiving from week to week or month to month? What could you do instead?

Stock Market

If you invested the money in the stock market, you'd see the income initially was a bit less than you would have received on deposit. Then you would see it catch up and begin to rise steadily. After twenty years, you're getting about five or six times more income from the stocks than you are from deposits. What is this income we're talking about? It's income that arose from the FT Actuaries All-Share Index.

You might say this doesn't make any sense. The stock markets collapsed and so on. Shares have been going up and down. How could this make any sense?

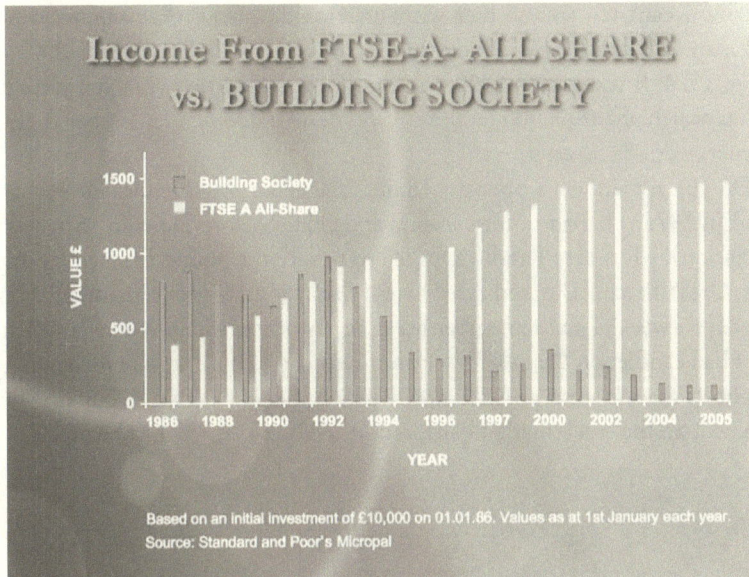

Well, it does. What I'm talking about here is the income that arose from those shares, not the value of the capital. The capital goes up and down, but the dividends keep increasing. If you look at the FTSE 100 Share Index as well as the 250, 350, and 750 All-Share Index, what you find is that 93 per cent of all those companies in the index keep increasing their dividends. So you keep getting more income. As long as you leave the capital value there for long enough to care for itself, guess what happens? It does.

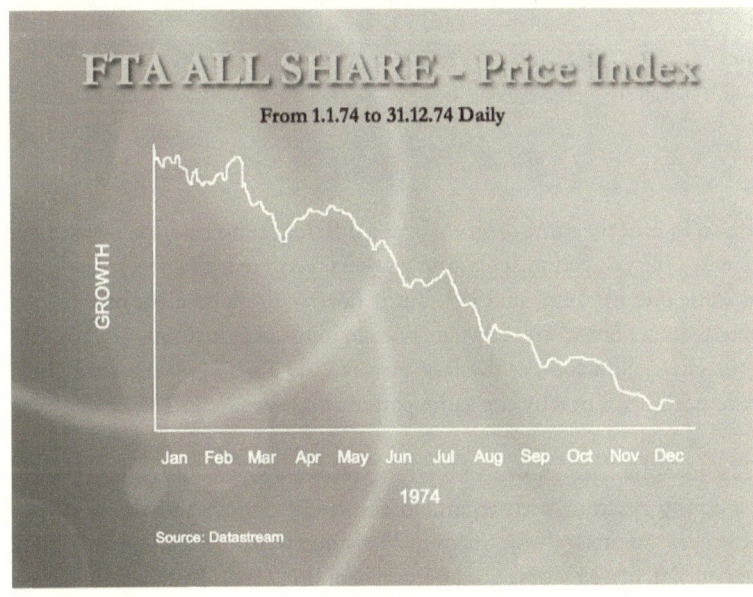

Now I can't tell you all that without reminding you what happened to the stock market back in 1974. If you think it was bad in 2001, 2002, or 2003, look back to 1974. If you put £10,000 into the stock market that year, you were lucky if it was worth about £2,000 by the end of the year. Do you remember that? The first energy crisis caused it?

Do you remember a previous labour chancellor, Mr Dennis Healey, at the airport in 1974? He had to turn around and come back to Downing Street as the International Monetary Fund was called in to save the pound from collapsing. In effect, Great Britain Limited nearly went bankrupt. Do you remember working three days a week? I can remember being in my office, which was in Ilford at the time. I had candles on the desk. I wore my overcoat because we had no heating and no light. It doesn't seem possible now when you look back on it, but that's what happened. So the stock market collapsed. It fell by 83 per cent to be precise.

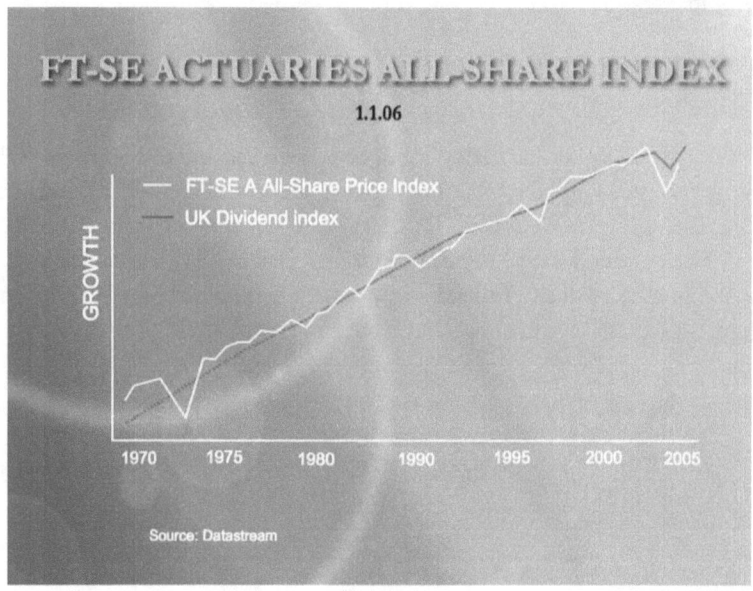

If you look at the same diagram over a different timescale, look what happens. There was a big correction. Then the markets recovered. The stock market fell by 40 per cent one weekend in 1987, but it doesn't show here because the market recovered. Such blips won't affect medium to long-term investments. You can't see it on the chart. Now look at the last few years. The market went down, but then it recovered. This is exactly the same pattern that we saw in 1974 being repeated here.

The markets have shown very strong recovery since 2003, though there has been a strong reaction with regard to the credit crunch and the high price of oil. However, markets always recover. How many people reading this book can remember that, fifteen years ago, a million people in Great Britain were in negative equity in property? So people held onto their properties until they recovered. They waited. The recovery came through, and now their property prices have gone up.

The recent credit crunch has caused severe problems both for the world's stock markets and the world's property markets. The position with regard to "subprime mortgages" in the USA has been well documented, and I don't think I need to go into great detail with regard to how this has happened and why. The principle, however, with regard to markets is that they always, always, always recover. Whenever there are difficult times, my clients always tell me 'Yes, John, but it's different this time.' But it isn't! In my thirty-five years as a financial adviser, I always say it is just shades of a spectrum. There have always been corrections in the past, and there will always be corrections in the future. The time to invest is always when the markets have been down before they recover. Most clients wait until the market recovers and reaches the top before they have the courage to invest, and this is the wrong way round!

The Magic Formula

What's the magic formula that drives this and keeps it going? Imagine a sweatshirt made by a supermarket that sold back in 1975 for £3.99. Now I know there are cheap Chinese imports and things have come down a bit. Actually, what's happened over the period is that prices have increased. Back in 1975, it sold for £3.99 with raw material and labour costs, distribution overheads, and a profit margin. Back then, our friends, the supermarket, made about 30 per cent. That means they made a £1 profit. What did they do with this profit? They gave their workers a pay rise, bought some new plant and machinery, opened a new store somewhere, and paid a dividend to their shareholders.

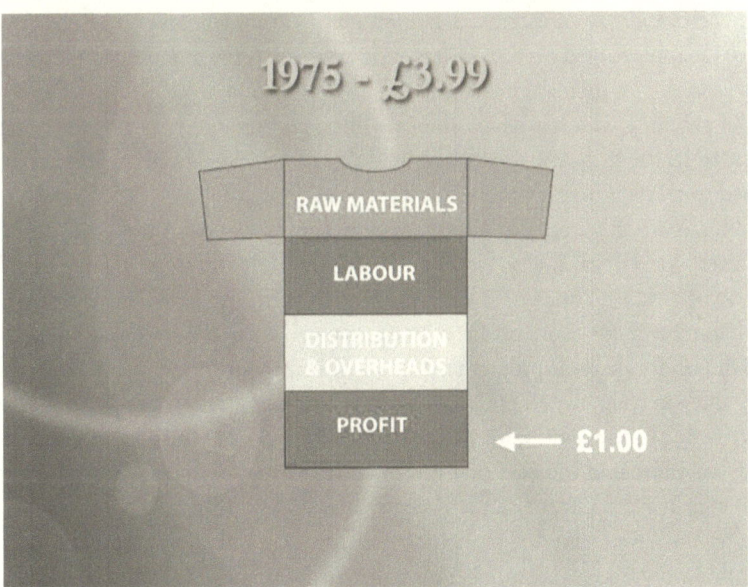

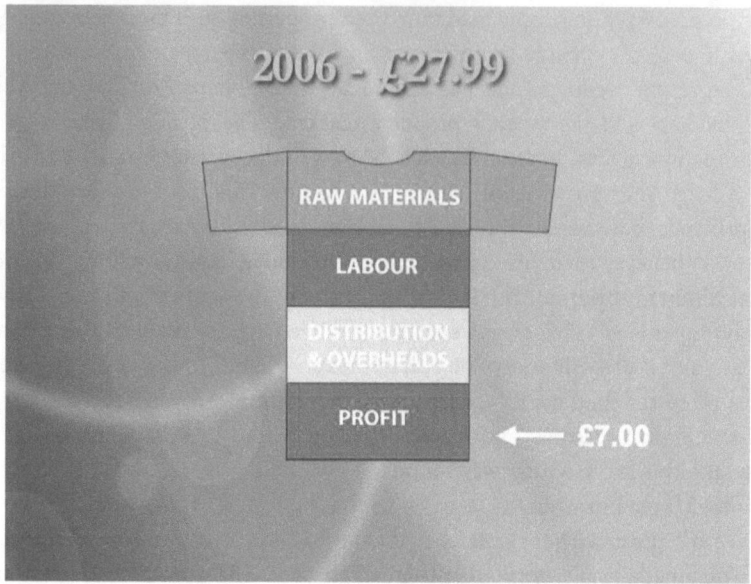

Despite the fact that this sweatshirt is coming in from China, it still costs more than it did twenty-five years ago. Now the same sweatshirt is £27.99. It's still made up of raw material and labour costs, distribution overheads, and profit margins. The supermarkets still make about 30 per cent. So now they make a £7 profit, which is seven times the profit they were making thirty-three years ago. What does the supermarket do with this greatly enhanced profit? They give their workers a pay rise, buy some new plant and machinery, open a new superstore somewhere, and pay an increased dividend to their shareholders. The chairman of Tesco was interviewed on the TV recently because Tesco announced their figures. These showed an increase in their dividend.

So anybody who has Tesco shares will be getting a letter from the company chairman in the next few weeks saying, 'Well done! Here's a bit more money. I'm pleased to tell you that it's more than last year.'

This is a microcosm of Great Britain Limited and all the companies you have ever worked for. The value of goods when it left the factory gate costs more because of inflation. Because it costs more, your company made more profit. So, as your company made more profit, it could give you a pay raise and pay an increased dividend on its shares. I predict that this will continue.

Now you could say to me that China is producing cheap goods, so it changes everything. That's absolutely true. Has anybody looked at the cost of a motor car? Have you compared the cost of a motor car to what it was ten, fifteen, or twenty years ago? It's not cheaper. It still costs more. Most things still cost more. But some things have come down, including electronics and computers. But, with the cost of oil now rising and things going up, we're under inflationary pressures, and it's why we expect to see inflation go higher. And it's fair to assume that these sweatshirts in the supermarket will cost more at some time in the future than they cost today. So the supermarket will make more profit, so they can give you more increase in their dividends.

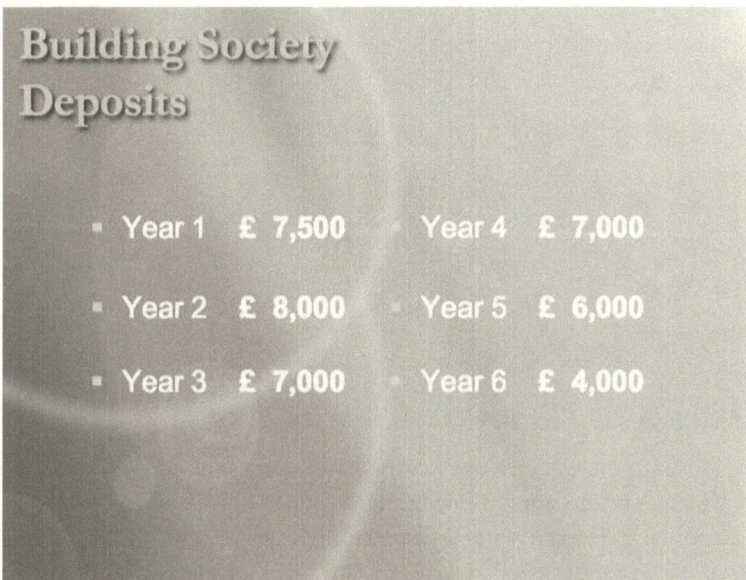

Building Society Deposits

- Year 1 £ 7,500
- Year 2 £ 8,000
- Year 3 £ 7,000
- Year 4 £ 7,000
- Year 5 £ 6,000
- Year 6 £ 4,000

Suppose I wanted to offer you a job. You would start off at £7,500 a year. After you've worked for me for six years, I'll only pay you £4,000 per year. How many of you would come and work for me on that basis? I should think that not many of you would. But, if you've retired and had £100,000 on deposit in a bank or a building society, that's the return you've accepted from it with interest rates ranging from 7.5 per cent to 4 per cent over the last six years. You won't come and work for me, but you'll retire and put your money to work. And that's what you'll accept from it. Remember … stop accumulating and start spending!

Key Questions

4. How much money have you invested in banks, building societies, national savings certificates, and gilts?
5. How much money have you invested for your nursing care?
6. What kind of income are you looking for? Up-and-down income? Level income? Rising income?

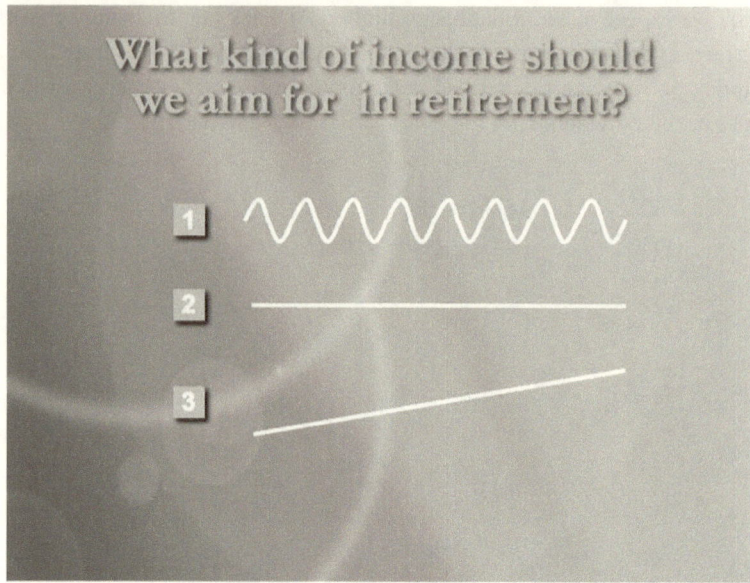

What sort of income are you looking for in retirement? Do you want up-and-down income, level income, or rising income?

Everybody dislikes the up-and-down income; they want rising income. Up-and-down income is our bank and building society. Level income is gilts. Rising income is from shares. That's what most of my clients tell me they want when they retire. If nothing else, they need it to keep up with inflation.

Put Your Eggs in Different Baskets

The wise, sensible, prudent investor has different eggs in different baskets. But, there are four main investment areas that apply to everyone: property, the stock market (equities), gilts (government securities), and cash.

Most people get this equation wrong. Let's assume your estate is worth £500,000. You have a property worth £250,000. The rest of your investment is £250,000 in different areas. In my experience, by putting your property to one side, most people will have about 80 per cent in gilts and cash and only about 20 per cent in the stock market. It's the wrong way around. It should be about 70 per cent in the stock market and only about 30 per cent in cash and gilts. The next chapter will show you more specific strategies for achieving this mix of investments.

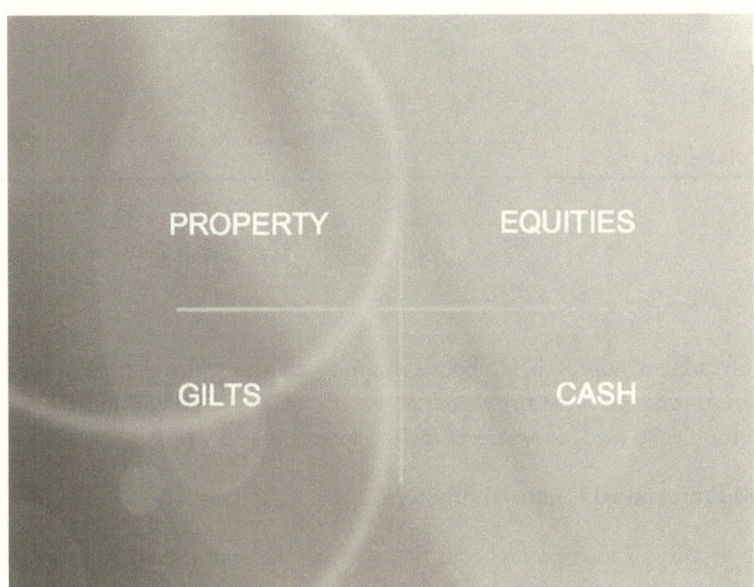

Chapter Four

What Is Your Investment Strategy?

My investment approach is about designing an investment strategy for each individual that gives security and peace of mind as well as making use of opportunities to save tax wherever those opportunities exist.

Hire a Professional Financial Adviser

Most people go to a professional financial adviser like myself to spread their money around because they don't know how to play the investment game.

Managed Funds: Spreading the Risk and Increasing the Reward

A professional financial adviser will take that money and put it into investment funds called managed funds, which have very special tax advantages.

The idea of investing in managed funds is very simple. You go to your adviser and tell him how much capital you have available. He will arrange to put it into a managed fund for you. Better still, he will put it in several managed funds for you. So the idea here is that, if you have five fund managers and they are spreading the money around into the stock market, property, government securities, and cash, you end up with twenty different eggs in twenty different baskets. This would be referred to as a widespread, defensive investment portfolio strategy. It doesn't mean it can't go down. It will go down if markets go wrong, but it should come back up when markets rise. It should protect the value of your investment over the medium- to long-term future. But it does mean that, over the medium- to long-term future, you should expect to get a real return on that money, especially ahead of inflation.

Financial advisers are always thrilled when their clients' investment returns are good. I particularly like to see my clients when the investments I've made are making good profits for them. Clients are always very happy when you are. But you do have to accept you get periods of volatility. That's why spreading your investments across a number of fund managers gives you that security. It means you're not putting all your eggs in one particular basket.

In the United Kingdom, these types of investments are always referred to as investment bonds, which is different to most other parts of the world. In the United States, they are usually referred to as mutual funds.

Tax Advantages of Managed Investment Bonds

So the idea is to put you into a managed investment bond with tax advantages. Here's the first one.

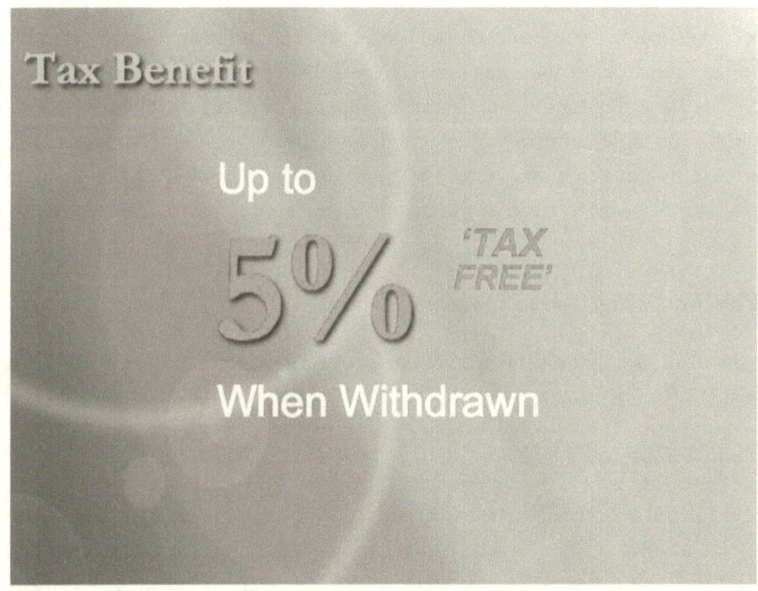

Tax Benefit

Up to

5% 'TAX FREE'

When Withdrawn

You can take 5 per cent income tax-free in any tax year. So, if you were a client of mine, you could say to me, 'Here's my £10,000, John, does that mean I can have £500 a year tax-free?' I would say, 'Yes, you can have it quarterly, half-yearly, or even monthly if you prefer.'

Therefore, if you were to invest £100,000 into this type of investment bond, irrespective of whether you are a basic rate tax payer in the UK or a high rate tax payer, you could take £5,000 per annum in tax-free income, and it doesn't even have to be put on your UK tax returns. And the good news is that there is no tax to pay on this.

The fund managers deduct the basic rate so you, as an individual, have no personal liability to basic rate tax. It is only if you are a higher rate tax payer at the time the investment is surrendered that there may be a potential high rate tax charge, but, with sensible tax planning, this can be avoided.

Clients often ask if they can draw down this 5 per cent, say, in one, three, or five years, and the answer is that you could, and you might want to use it for when you go into a nursing home. The 5 per cent allowance accumulates each year so that after five years you could draw a 25 per cent lump sum tax-free.

Many of my clients give me money to invest now. Then they start to draw down from this capital when they need long-term health or nursing care fees.

Clients often worry about withdrawing the 5 per cent and the effect this might have on their capital. In a bad year, if you withdraw 5 per cent and the fund makes 3 per cent, you would be losing 2 per cent of your capital. However, there are more good years than bad. As long as the fund makes more than 5 per cent on average and covers the annual management charge of the fund manager, you will be ahead of the game. In my thirty-five years of experience of arranging this type of investment, I can honestly say that, over the medium- to long-term basis, I have never had a client who has lost money utilising this investment philosophy.

So it's very flexible and designed to be so. You have the income when you want it, for example, monthly, quarterly, or annually. You defer it, spend it, increase it, decrease it, stop it, or start it at any time. Put the money in. Then just draw it down at some specified time in the future to meet some particular requirement.

So Why Would You Use a Financial Adviser?

A financial adviser can help you to make long-term investments by not putting all your eggs into one basket.

No Commission to Pay

Some financial advisers allocate 100 per cent of your funds to units at the bid price with no initial charges. The bid price is simply the price you surrender units at in a fund. It's different if you are dealing with banks, building societies, and independent financial advisers because they normally charge you at least a 5 per cent initial fee, which is their commission. This is made up by investing your units at the offer price, not the bid price. The offer price is simply the price at which units are offered to you by the insurance or investment company. This 5 per cent differential on charge is paid as initial commission. The fund manager will then make an average annual charge of 1.5 per cent of the funds under management. That is how the fund manager gets paid.

Other institutions, such as St. James's Place, do not deal with banks, building societies, or independent financial advisers. This makes a big difference to you because 100 per cent of your money is invested at the bid price. The only charge is the annual 1.5 per cent management charge.

This means that, when you deal with someone like me and St. James's Place, your buying price for your units and your selling price of your units are the same. Provided you leave the investment for six years, there is no initial charge. There is no additional charge if you take advantage of the 5 per cent tax-free withdrawal facility. However, if you surrender all the investment before six years, then an early exit charge will apply as follows:

Years	Early Exit Charge (%)
6	Nil
5	1
4	2
3	3
2	4
1	5
0	6

Putting all of your money to work

For Long Term Investment

- Allocate 100% of your monies to units

- At the bid price

- So NO initial charge

Note:
An early exit charge will be incurred if the bond is surrendered within six years.

Funds Are Monitored

Most institutions monitor their fund managers. They may meet the company six times a year and review the funds. How are we doing? How are our competitors doing? Are they doing better than us? If they are, why are they doing better than us? What are they doing that we're not doing? If we're doing better than them, why are we doing better than them? What are we doing that they're not doing?

If the fund managers don't perform, they are replaced by fund managers who do. They move that money around. The 1.5 per cent annual management charge covers all of this. You don't get charged any extra for this. If they change fund managers, that's all done automatically. There's no capital gains tax, income tax, and charge for doing it. That's part of the service you get when you deal with someone like myself.

Inheritance Tax Savings

As you'll see, all of these schemes can be linked to an inheritance tax scheme to get the money outside of your estate. So why would you go into a scheme like this to save inheritance tax and then cash it all in? However, the fact is that you can if you want to.

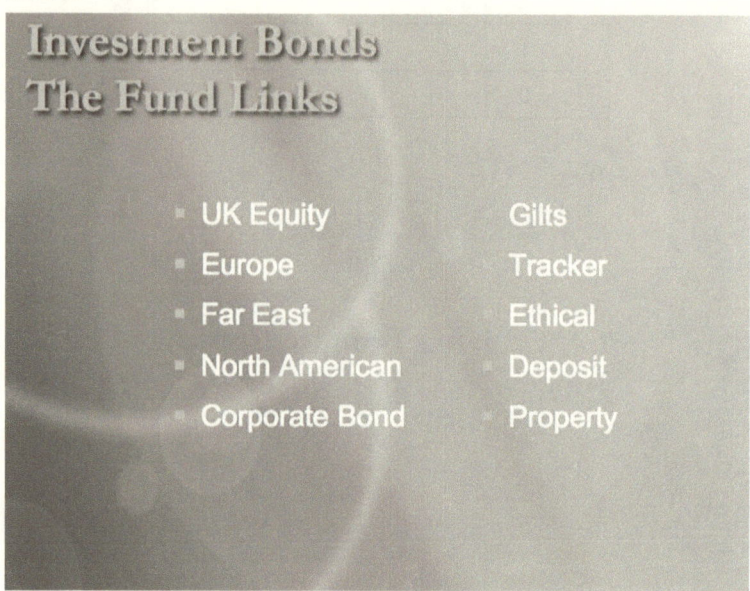

**Investment Bonds
The Fund Links**

- UK Equity
- Europe
- Far East
- North American
- Corporate Bond

- Gilts
- Tracker
- Ethical
- Deposit
- Property

More Choice of Investments

You don't have to have just managed funds. Companies have a whole range of funds. So you could say to me, 'Well, John, I hear what you say, but I'm still worried about equities. I'm worried about the stock market. What I'd really like is 100 per cent of my money in property. Can you arrange for me to have 100 per cent of my investment in property?'

I would say, 'Yes, we can.'

Then you would say, 'Or in gilts or an ethical fund. I like ethical funds. I don't want to deal with these people who sell tobacco, spirits, and all that sort of stuff.'

So you can actually dictate. You can say to me, 'I want to decide my own mixture rather than you decide for me. Can I do that?'

I say, 'Absolutely.'

Most clients don't. They're very happy to let their adviser do it for them, but you do have the choice. And, up to twice a year, you can switch and move the money around free of charge if you wish to do so. If you do it more than twice a year, then there's a £25 admin charge. So, in relative terms, it's nothing.

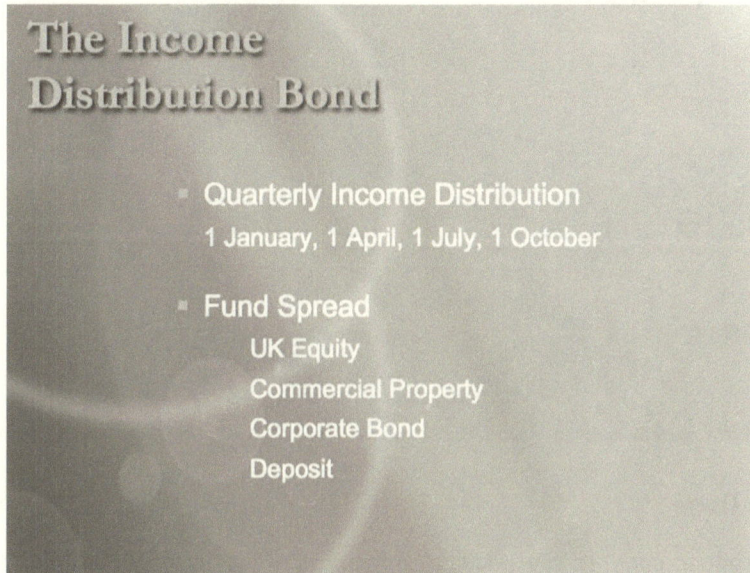

The Income Distribution Bond

- Quarterly Income Distribution
  1 January, 1 April, 1 July, 1 October

- Fund Spread
  UK Equity
  Commercial Property
  Corporate Bond
  Deposit

Distribution Bonds

The funds in which you invest are run by financial institutions who specialise in managing clients investments. I am sure that you are aware that, in the UK, we have a huge number of financial institutions and insurance companies who arrange investments. With the distribution bond, these various institutions that you invest in pay all the income that they've earned in that particular quarter. They will spread your capital into UK equity, commercial property, and corporate bonds. Again, if you deal with St. James's Place and myself, there will be no initial commission charge.

I'll explain later how all of these bonds can be used to save substantial amounts of inheritance tax.

Unit Trusts

Growth	Income
• Far East	UK High Income
• Greater European Progressive	Corporate Bond
• International	Equity Income
• North American	
• UK and General Progressive	
• Recovery	
• Ethical	
• Tracker	

Unit Trusts

Depending upon if you want a growth portfolio, income portfolio, or a combination of both, lots of funds are available. Basically, unit trusts are stock market investments into various equities. Each individual fund manager will put together a number of equities to produce a particular portfolio that is designed to meet your investment needs. In the UK, the present government has made this type of investment much more attractive by offering individual savings accounts (ISAs). Essentially, all unit trusts in the UK are now available in ISA form.

It is still possible, however, to split your ISA into two parts: a cash component of £3,000 and an equity component of £4,000. So the maximum amount that can be invested into an ISA is currently £7,000. This has been increased to £7,200 in tax year 2008. Alternatively, if you do not wish to utilise the cash element of your ISA, you may also invest this into the stock market into equities, so all of the £7,000 can be invested into a unit trust.

Who'd Like to Be a Millionaire?

Well, you probably all would. You probably all are. But, essentially, £75,000 invested twenty-one years ago in our oldest trust, our European fund, is valued at £1.69 million today. Our international fund is valued at £1.1 million. Remember that includes all the ups and downs in the meantime. So here's a pretty good idea if you'd like me to make a £1 million for you. Would you give me £75,000?

Who'd be a Millionaire

£75,000 invested twenty one years ago in our oldest unit trusts.

FUND	CURENT VALUE
SJP Greater European Progressive	£1.69M
SJP International	£1.10M

Past performance is not necessarily a guide to the future.
Prices can go down as well as up.

Source: Lipper Hindsight
Offer to offer reinvested, 30.09.84 to 30.12.05.
Five year performance 29.12.00 to 30.12.05. SJP Greater European £87,805,
SJP International £95,313

Leave it with me for about twenty-five years in one of these two funds. With a bit of luck, we will turn it into £1 million for you! Really, this just makes the point about long-term investment and how well this can work for you if you will let it.

Individual Savings Accounts

A lot of people say ISAs are terrible, but they're not. ISAs are great. Probably the fund you linked it to in 2000, 2001, or 2002 was terrible because you picked one of these high-tech Internet funds and you lost a lot of money. I've seen people today who've lost 90 per cent of their value, but ISAs, in principle, are good. The Chancellor has said he'll allow them for the next ten years. Remember you can put £7,000 a year in. Spouses, you can put in £7,000. (From tax year April 2008, this will be increased to £7,200.) As a married couple, that's £14,000. (For tax year 2008, it will be £14,400.) For the next ten years, that's £144,000 you can get invested. I say they're tax-free, of course, but that's not quite true. The dividend now is taxed, and there is a sting in the tail with ISAs and your personal equity plans (PEPs).

The Chancellor has told you that they're not subject to tax, but, of course, they are, aren't they? All of them are subject to inheritance tax. Many of you are sitting on PEPs and ISAs worth £50,000, £60,000, and £100,000, all for the benefit of the government. They are really pleased about it because they are going to have 40 per cent of all that lot when you die.

ISA Rules

I'm sure most people know all the rules, but many people are getting confused as to what the ISA rules are.

Example One

A lady I saw recently said she'd done her ISA. I assumed she'd invested £7,000. Later during the discussion, I realised she'd only invested £3,000 into a cash ISA. That doesn't mean you can't have a £4,000 equity ISA to make it up to £7,000. There's nothing to stop you. You can either put £7,000 into equity ISA, £3,000 into cash ISA, and another £4,000 into an equity ISA. So be aware of that one because some people are missing this.

You can only have one ISA in a year, but it's possible to go to an institution who offer eight different fund managers. So, if you wish, this means you can go across one or all eight of those investments.

You can also spread it across the different fund managers so you've got different eggs in different baskets.

Many of you have got ISAs. You may not be happy with the present fund performance, and you may want to change that. You could talk to me about a PEP transfer or an ISA transfer where we will transfer you from your existing funds and invest into a multi-manager. So, if you wish, you can invest into all these different fund managers. By transferring your investment, it does not lose its PEP or ISA status.

There are only two reasons why you should consider a transfer. One, you're not happy with the present fund managers. You're not being looked after. You're not receiving any advice, guidance, service, or anything like that, and you want to do something with it. Second, you want to increase your income.

Example Two

A few months ago, one client complained about being squeezed on income. He and his wife had about £100,000 in PEPs, and he wasn't taking any income from them. I suggested switching them into a monthly income portfolio, which was roughly paying 4 per cent a year net. That meant he could have a tax-free income of £330 a month straight away. So he transferred it from his existing PEP and put it into a monthly income portfolio PEP. He and his wife are now receiving this extra income.

Remember that. Most of you have capital growth situations. Your investments are only accumulating inside your estate for the benefit of the Inland Revenue. Start to utilise them. Give yourself some benefit so you can enjoy the money and spend the income.

Simplify Your Life

Most people feel overwhelmed by the complexity of their investments. They have shares they have inherited or shares they have bought. These include privatisations, British Telecom, British Gas, and similar. They want to really tidy up and sort them all out. This is where a share exchange can help.

Share Exchange

Maybe you have become tired of the paperwork. That naturally happens as you age. You've had great fun doing it for the last twenty, thirty, forty, or fifty years, but now you don't want the hassle anymore. You want to spend your time enjoying yourself.

Example Three

Eighteen months ago, one of my clients had a stroke, rang me up, and said, 'John, I really can't cope with any of this anymore. Can you help me sort everything out so that, if anything happens to me, my wife's going to be okay and I haven't got to be thinking or worrying about it?'

I'm pleased to say that, in that gentleman's case, we took his shares and did a share exchange. We put them into investment bonds. Unfortunately, the gentleman died three months ago. However, because of what we did, everything was sorted out for his wife. There was nothing for her to worry about and nothing for her to get involved in. It was all sorted out before anything happened to that client. You should consider doing the same.

In summary, I would like to discuss the five key factors that I believe have impacted you in the last one, three, five, seven, and ten years. These are likely to impact you in the next several years.

Inflation

Since the Second World War, everyone reading this book will have experienced some form of inflation. It has become a way of life. We accept that prices do keep increasing. One only has to look at the price of oil and how much we now have to pay for our petroleum to realise just what an effect that inflation can have. I think most people will accept that we are likely to have some form of inflation built into the system, but I do occasionally meet one or two people who forecast deflation or stagnation. However, most of us know that we will have to pay more for goods and services in the future compared with the prices we paid in the past. From an investment viewpoint, this means the value of assets needs to be invested to stay ahead of whatever the current rate of inflation is. Another very important point is that, if inflation does continue for the next five, ten, or twenty years, the value of the assets we all own will increase. Therefore, they will attract more inheritance tax.

Fluctuating Interest Rates

Interest rates have fluctuated ever since time began. This is not likely to be any different in the future. The only question is as to whether interest rates will be higher in the future or lower than they are currently. As I write this book, interest rates have peaked at just above 5 per cent. Although one or two forecasters see interest rates at slightly higher levels, I have seen no forecasts from London or anywhere else in the world suggesting that interest rates over the next ten years or so are likely to go back up to the levels of 15 per cent or more that were seen previously.

No Capital Growth in the Banks nor Building Societies

As pointed out in my earlier illustration, whoever invests capital into a bank or building society does not receive capital growth on his or her investment. He or she simply receives the interest that the institution pays. The person who makes the capital growth is the person who borrows your money, buys a property with it in your area, and then sells it for a substantial profit at some time in the future. By investing into banks and building societies, you have cut yourself off from one of two ways in which money grows, that is, through income appreciation or capital appreciation.

Increasing Dividends Every Year

It is an historical fact that dividends have increased year after year, irrespective of the capital value of stock markets. Yes, there are periods when dividends may not go up as fast as they have done previously. There are always companies that will not increase their dividend, but they at least maintain it. However, overall dividends do increase. You only have to look at the FTSE 100, 250, 350, and 750 to see evidence of that over any measurable periods of time that you care to mention.

In the last ten years, the dividends paid by companies in the FTSE 100 share index have more than doubled. In simple language, if you were receiving £5,000 in dividends ten years ago from your investments and if you hold the same investments today, you will now be receiving at least £10,000 in dividend payments. If you go back twenty years, you will find dividend payments have, on average, more than quadrupled.

Stock Market Values Increase over the Long-term Basis

Stock market values certainly do increase over the long-term basis, but it may not seem like it, especially since 2001 and the terrorist attacks. However, although the markets fell substantially during 2001, 2002, and 2003, they have since recovered strongly. And they will continue to do so in the future. I am always brave enough to stand up to be counted and suggest the FTSE 100 Share Index will go through 7000. It most certainly will. It is simply a question of when. Unfortunately, I don't know the day when it will happen. I just know it will. That is how the markets work.

FT-SE 1st January Each Year

Year	Value	Change	Year	Value	Change
1989	1793.10		1998	5135.00	+24.69%
1990	2434.10	+35.00%	1999	5882.60	+14.50%
1991	2128.30	- 12.48%	2000	6931.00	+17.82%
1992	2492.80	+17.10%	2001	6221.00	- 10.20%
1993	2846.50	+14.12%	2002	5217.40	- 16.10%
1994	3408.00	+19.72%	2003	3940.00	- 24.50%
1995	3065.50	- 10.04%	2004	4477.00	+13.60%
1996	3689.00	+20.30%	2005	4814.00	+ 7.50%
1997	4118.00	+11.62%	2006	5618.80	+16.70%

+ 8.20%

Plus Dividends 3%

TOTAL AVERAGE RETURN   11.2%

Look at the FT-SE 100, the one you're most familiar with. Here, you'll see something kind of interesting. There's only been five negative years in the last seventeen. It just so happens that three of those negative years came between 2001 and 2003. So it seems like it's always been down. No, we just had three bad years together. But, since then, the market has recovered. Where have you been investing your money while the market has been going up? You would have made 13.6 per cent in 2004, 7.5 per cent in 2005, and 16.7 per cent in 2006. That's a total of 37.8 per cent. In addition to that, there have been dividends of about 3 per cent, so the average return over that period has been 12.45 per cent, 9.45 per cent on the FTSE, and another 3 per cent dividend. The overall average since 1989, which includes all the highs and lows, is 8.2 per cent plus dividends of 3 per cent, a total average return of 11.2 per cent. Is this rate of return going to continue? Yes, it is. Is the market going to continue to improve? Yes, it is. There are many reasons why, but, basically, the fundamental principles are all in line to make the markets go up over the medium- to long-term future despite the present uncertainties.

We certainly see the market going into higher ground, back up and ahead of 7000. The FTSE 100 will get back to that 7000 figure eventually. I can't tell you the day, week, or month, but that's the way markets work. The markets are recovering. They are already 2700 points from the low point since 2001. Prior to the war in Iraq, the FTSE 100 was 3200. This means that the market has recovered by over 3000 points since the low point. That's a massive gain over that period, so take advantage of it.

Due to the credit crunch the market has already fallen to 3800 since I wrote the above comments, which may make my forecast seem perverse. However, in the medium to long term the market will recover and those clients that invest now will make real gains.

Key questions

7.   Is all of your money working for you?
8.   Are all your investment eggs in one basket?
9.   Who is advising you to spread your risk and increase your reward?

Part Two

Okay, I Can't Take It with Me. So Who Gets It?

Chapter Five

Headlines from the *Financial Mail* on January 19, 2007, stated, 'Millions will fall into inheritance tax trap.' Again, from the *Daily Express* on February 5, 2007, it read, '2.4 million face Brown's death tax mauling.'

Even though you can't take it with you when you die, you don't want your heirs and estate to lose out on your valuable assets. Based on my experience as a financial adviser, here are some recommendations for you to consider.

Rule One: The Law of Inertia

The terrible thing about inheritance tax is how much tax is being paid that need not be. According to a BBC TV survey from May 2006, in the tax year 2004/2005, the Chancellor collected £2.6 billion in inheritance tax. Of that £2.6 billion, £1.6 billion need not have been paid. In other words, 60 per cent of all the inheritance tax is currently being paid for one reason only. It's called the law of inertia. I must get round to this ... I must get round to this ... I must get round to this.

So let's look at what part of your estate isn't yours at all and what the Inland Revenue is waiting to come and take away from you. And I'm going to ask you to stop for a second and just read the next sentence a few times. This will be the largest tax bill you will ever pay. Think about that. Those of you who have paid some large tax bills along the way still have a bigger tax bill facing you. It's quite a sobering thought. I know what some of you are thinking, 'Well, I'm not going to pay it, John. The kids are. So there!'

All right, that is absolutely true. But here are some questions for you. Did you work hard and diligently all of your life? Did you pay tax at the basic rate, tax at the high rate, and capital gains tax? Despite all of that you managed to build up a decent estate, you're just going to give another 40 per cent of it all to the Chancellor when you die. Is that what you did it for?

Most people say, 'No, it isn't what I did it for. If I can legitimately utilise schemes that will enable me to get money outside of my estate and save inheritance tax on it so my children and grandchildren can inherit more, then that is something I'd like to do. Is that a reasonable situation to be in?' (Please note the use of the word 'legitimately.')

They are absolutely right. That's where most people are coming from.

Famous Quotes

Just before we go any further, I want to introduce you to one or two famous quotes. Our good friend Caesar Augustus said, 'Let all the world be taxed.' Ever since that day, there's been some sort of tax on all wealth in all societies. If you look in the *Doomsday Book*, you'll find it's 'oats and groats' and things like that. But the bottom line is that it's there.

'Inheritance tax, the voluntary tax.'

Who said that? Gordon Brown, previously the Chancellor and now Prime Minister, said it when he was in opposition. He's not saying that now, is he?

My favourite quote is, 'Inheritance tax is a voluntary levy paid by those who distrust their heirs more than they dislike the Inland Revenue.'

Isn't that wonderful? The late Roy Jenkins said that in 1986 when inheritance tax was first introduced in the Finance Act that year. This was the quote he actually used in the House during the budget debate.

'One is not getting their hands on one's jewels.' I'm told this is absolutely quite genuine, but one does have to accept it is hearsay because it was reported by a person who was an insider at Buckingham Palace.

Her Majesty Queen Elizabeth II said this in June 2002 when she famously did a deal with the Inland Revenue to protect the royal family in the future from some of the ravages of inheritance tax.

But many people don't realise that, when Diana, Princess of Wales died, she had received a settlement from Prince Charles following their divorce. However, because no serious tax planning had been done, over £8 million in inheritance tax was paid on her estate. Now you would have thought that the Royal Family would have access to some wonderful financial advice? Unfortunately, as mentioned earlier, due to the law of inertia, they just didn't get around to it. None of us know the day, minute, or hour we will die. That is why it is so important to plan ahead, particularly with regard to inheritance tax.

Rule Two: Your Villa in Spain Is Liable for Tax

This applies if you pay your taxes in the UK. The bad news is that everything in the estate is potentially liable to tax. That means what it says. When I did a seminar a few years ago, a gentleman asked if this included his villa in Spain. We had to give him a glass of water and bring him round when I told him it did! He thought, because his villa was in Spain, he was out of the UK tax net. Wrong. Your villa in Spain, your condominium in America, your sheep farm in Australia, your ski lodge in Switzerland, and your offshore investments will all be part of your estate for inheritance tax purposes. It is absolutely 100 per cent certain.

Rule Three: Die Abroad!

There is only one legal way to avoid paying inheritance tax. You must die abroad and stay dead abroad. Now that doesn't mean you can go to France on a day trip, die, and solve your problem. It means that you move away completely from the UK and have no assets here whatsoever.

The famous case of Sir Richard Burton confirms this. When Sir Richard died, his will specifically stated his wish to be buried in the Welsh mountains. In fact, he is not buried in the Welsh mountains. He's buried in Switzerland with a piece of Welsh granite over his grave. Why? The answer is very simple. The moment the aeroplane carrying his coffin touched the tarmac at Heathrow, his entire estate would have become liable to UK inheritance tax.

Rule Four: Ducking and Diving Doesn't Work

Now one of the things I've observed about my friends, clients, and people like you who are reading this book is the game they play with regard to inheritance tax. This is very similar to something I observed many years ago when I used to have a Labrador bitch called Sally. It was the first Labrador bitch I'd had. She came into season for the first time.

My next-door neighbour, who had a very old dog, said, 'Well, you won't have any problem with him. He's well past it.'

His dog got under the fence, over the fence, around the fence, across the fence, through the fence, and between the fence. We came down one morning to find he'd dug a trench literally under the fence to get at my Sally.

What's that got to do with you and your inheritance tax? Everything. You try and find a way—around the tax, over the tax, through the tax, between the tax, under the tax, and across the tax. You're all trying it. Don't you think that, if it was possible to do all these things, we'd all be doing it? But I see clients every single week who are trying all these dodges, 'ducking and diving' and 'bobbing and weaving.' Trust me, I'm a financial adviser. It doesn't work. You can't do these things.

> ## Treasury Commissioned Survey
>
> " £2.9 Billion paid in Inheritance Tax in 2004/5"
>
> *of which*
>
> "£1.6 Billion could have been avoided"
>
> *by*
>
> "careful tax planning, seeking proper advice"

Rule Five: Plan to Pay Your Tax Bill

When are you going to have to pay this tax? Well, you're either going to pay it on a death of a single person or the surviving spouse in a normal marriage. In the last tax year, this was £2.9 billion. Who paid this £2.9 billion? Of course, this wasn't all of you because you are still alive. However, these are the people who have died who came to my seminar last year, the year before, and the year before that. All of those people are paying this. As I said to you earlier, £1.6 billion need not have been paid by just incorporating careful tax planning and seeking proper advice. That's why I'm advising you to seek advice on careful tax planning.

How much tax are you going to pay then? Remember that it includes your home. Now let's have a look what the government has announced. Prior to the general election in 2005, the Chancellor was feeling extremely generous when he announced figures on 17 March 2005, 'For the tax year 2005/6, the nil rate band will be £275,000. It's going up to £285,000 next year and, by the year 2007/8, will be increasing to £300,000.'

Since then, in his budget in March 2006, he has announced that the rates will be increased to £312,000 for 2008 and 2009 and £325,000 for 2010 onwards. How generous is that? In this current tax year, each one of you reading this book will pay £4,800 less than you would have done. In three years, you will pay £18,800 less than you would have done. That's pretty good, isn't it? How much do you think your property alone would increase over the same period?

Most of the clients I see in the UK tell me their property values have at least doubled over the last ten years. This means that a large amount, if not all, of their property will now be subject to inheritance tax, which it wouldn't have been ten years ago. This means the Chancellor, whoever he is, is always going to be well ahead of the game, isn't he? Perhaps the cleverest Chancellor of all was Mr Gordon Brown before he became Prime Minister. He invented ways of getting tax that nobody ever dreamed existed.

Your Estate

Let's have a look at your estate. Just suppose your estate was to grow by 7 per cent and the nil rate band grows by 3 per cent. Where have those figures come from? That's the actual performance of the last ten years according to the government's own actuaries. These figures were announced at the beginning of 2007. So, in the last ten years, most people's estates have grown on average by 7 per cent per annum compound. The Chancellor's inheritance tax allowance has increased by 3 per cent. So let's see how that might affect some of you reading this book.

How your estate could increase over time

Assuming your estate grows at 7% pa compound and a growth in the Nil Rate Band (currently £285,000) of 3% pa compound

Example 1

	Value of Estate	Inheritance Tax Bill
Current	£300,000	£6,000
In 5 years	£420,765	£36,148
In 10 years	£590,145	£82,851

Example One

Here's an estate currently valued at £750,000. The amount of tax payable on that is £60,000, but look at what's going to happen in five years and then ten years. This same estate in five years, only allowing for 7 per cent growth, will now be worth £1,052,000. Look what's happened to the inheritance tax. It has more than doubled. Now let's look at it for ten years. You will see that your estate has increased in value to £1,475,000. The inheritance tax is now £252,000. That is more than four times the amount of tax payable today.

How your estate could increase over time

Assuming your estate grows at 7% pa compound and a growth in the Nil Rate Band
(currently £285,000) of 3% pa compound

Example 2

	Value of Estate	Inheritance Tax Bill
Current	£400,000	£46,000
In 5 years	£561,020	£92,250
In 10 years	£786,860	£161,537

Example Two

This time, your estate is worth £1 million. Remember that it includes your home. The amount of tax payable is currently £160,000. In ten years, the amount of tax payable is £452,000, almost three times the amount of tax payable today.

And I can promise you the government has done exactly the same sums that we have done. The Chancellor has calculated his future inheritance tax in just the same way as I have here. This means that, despite the recent improvements and the utilisation of the double nil rate band, the Labour Party will be collecting some £4 billion in inheritance tax in five years. This does leave me to say that one shouldn't believe any politician and whichever party who says, 'If you vote for me, we will get rid of inheritance tax.' Where are they going to replace £4 billion in five years?

The Tory proposal to increase the nil rate band to £1 million would be an enormous advantage; however, it will still leave many estates with a considerable inheritance tax bill. They have come up with appropriate plans to tax non-domiciled persons to make up the shortfall on inheritance tax. Are you prepared to sit back and wait to see if the Conservative Party gets elected at the next election and risk that something might happen to you in the meantime? Or are you going to do some sensible tax planning now that will take care of the problem now and in the future, no matter what either political party decides to do?

It is a really horrendous tax. For most of you reading this book, it's probably true to say that, if I had written this book ten years ago, you might not have needed to read what I had to say about investments and inheritance tax planning. However, that's not true now.

Remember to think of your capital as a reservoir to be used.

Key Questions

10. Do you know how much inheritance tax you are going to pay?
11. Do you know how to save inheritance tax?
12. Do you have properties abroad?
13. Have you made a will yet?

Chapter Six

The Nitty-gritty—The Probate Challenge

Your estate comprises of your assets, including your home, investments, and all your worldly goods. After you die, your family want to inherit your estate, but they can't because a giant brick wall is between them and the inheritance. The giant brick wall is called probate. Probate is the legal definition of what will happen to your estate once you have died. Your estate is wound up, and your assets will be distributed as per your instructions, which are normally contained in your will. Probate will not be granted until the tax has been paid.

So your family can't go to Inland Revenue and say, 'Excuse me, if you let us take the property, we'll sell the property and pay the tax.'

'No,' says the Inland Revenue, 'you don't understand. You pay us the tax first. Then we give you probate. Then it's up to you what you do with the property.'

The Inland Revenue has just announced a special rule where they will allow you to take some cash or national savings certificate out of the estate, provided you're with what is called 'a participating bank or building society' and there is sufficient cash there to help meet the liability. But I've been helping clients meet estate liabilities for more than thirty-five years. After that period, I've had about one person who had enough money available to pay the inheritance tax that was due on the estate. Most people don't just leave substantial funds on deposit to meet the inheritance tax liability when they die. It's certainly not enough to meet the entire bill anyway.

For most people, probate is an absolute nightmare. You often can't get probate granted easily when there is an inheritance tax liability. Remember, if it's below the nil rate threshold, getting probate granted is very simple. It's not difficult. It takes a few months, but, if you're over the threshold, I can promise you that, on average, it takes at least a year and sometimes longer.

Examples

I saw a lady recently who told me that after six years, she still hadn't settled her father's estate.'

Another recent example was where a gentleman died and the estate was worth over £1 million, and after two years, it still had not been settled. This case involves a widow and two young children. So it can drag on for a long time.

In most of the cases I have been involved with over the last thirty-five years, there has never been enough money left in cash to meet the inheritance tax liability. This can cause a very real problem. Just how are the beneficiaries going to pay the tax if there isn't enough money to meet this liability? Usually, your beneficiaries will go to a bank and borrow some money, which, of course, they have to pay the interest on and then the tax man. But this can still take a year to eighteen months to sort out. Not only do your beneficiaries have to pay the tax, but they also have to pay the interest on the money they borrow.

Helping Your Family Meet the Probate Challenge

When my own father-in-law died, it took three years to get probate on his estate. Why? It wasn't his first marriage. He was a widower with two children. My mother-in-law was a widow with two children. It was wonderful that these two people met each other and then spent the next thirty years together. Unfortunately, however, Jack's children, who were my mother-in-law's stepchildren, challenged the will. That is why it took three years to get the estate settled.

Key Question

14. Do you have enough money invested to meet the probate challenge?

Five Options to Meet the Probate Challenge

(1) Utilise your allowances on death, which is now an automatic option.
(2) Consider giving some of your assets away whilst you're alive.
(3) Fund your liability with life assurance/life insurances.
(4) Put together a combination of these, whichever suits you and whichever you're comfortable with
(5) Do nothing ... and pay the price.

The 'Must Get Round to It' Option

One option you have and most of you are pursuing at present is doing nothing and, therefore, paying the price. You might say, 'You see, John, I must get round to it. I must get round to it. I must get round to it!'

Statistics quoted by the Probate Office in December 2006 show that seven people out of every ten people who die in Great Britain, die without making a will. Think about that for a second. For every hundred people who read this book, only thirty people have made a will. Why is this do you think? For many people, I believe that the day they sign the will is the first time they will ever have admitted in their lives that they are going to die. When they sign that piece of paper, it somehow or other seems as if they are tempting fate. Of course, this is nonsense, but this aspect of signing a will does bother people so they keep putting it off. If it makes anyone reading this book feel any better, a figure announced by the Law Society in March 2006, shows that five out of every ten solicitors who die don't have a will either!

If you do nothing and pay the price, that's up to you. I don't say you have to do anything. I just show you what the price is. If you want to pay it, that's entirely up to you. Assuming you wish to reduce your inheritance tax liability, however, let's see what sort of schemes are available and might be of help to you.

Key Question

15. How prepared are you to meet the probate challenge?

Utilise Your Allowances on Death

All the schemes I recommend have been available for a number of years. They are not new schemes that have suddenly appeared. The Inland Revenue has accepted them as inheritance tax saving schemes. I can say they do work and are acceptable to the Treasury. To use the modern parlance, 'It does what it says on the tin.' But one always has to be aware that the Inland Revenue can move the goalposts if they want to.

Having said that, precedents have been set over the years with regard to inheritance tax planning schemes. At the time of writing, I have had many clients who have taken out these schemes. When they subsequently died, there was no query from the Inland Revenue.

One important point to make is that neither I nor my company make a charge for setting up any of the schemes that I am going to discuss. My company makes an annual 1.5 per cent charge on the funds under management. That covers the cost of setting up all of the investments and inheritance tax schemes.

The Chancellor, Mr Darling, has done a lot to help with regard to reducing your inheritance tax by allowing the utilisation of the double nil rate band automatically, whether it was in your will or not. Everyone reading this book who is married or in a civil partnership will now receive £600,000 reduction on his or her estate. This will increase over the next few years until tax year 2009/2010 when the allowance will be £700,000. The starting point with regard to inheritance tax planning is always your will. By the way, if you haven't got a will, you do have one. It's called the government will, and it's based on the laws of intestacy. So let's start to see what could be done about the £300,000 nil rate tax band for tax year 2007/2008. You see, everybody has one of these £300,000 allowances.

Most men say to me, 'Oh, John I don't need to do anything because it goes to my wife anyway.'

I say, 'Nonsense, it does not.'

Here are the rules:

INTESTACY

Intestacy Rules - What happens to your estate when you die without making a will?

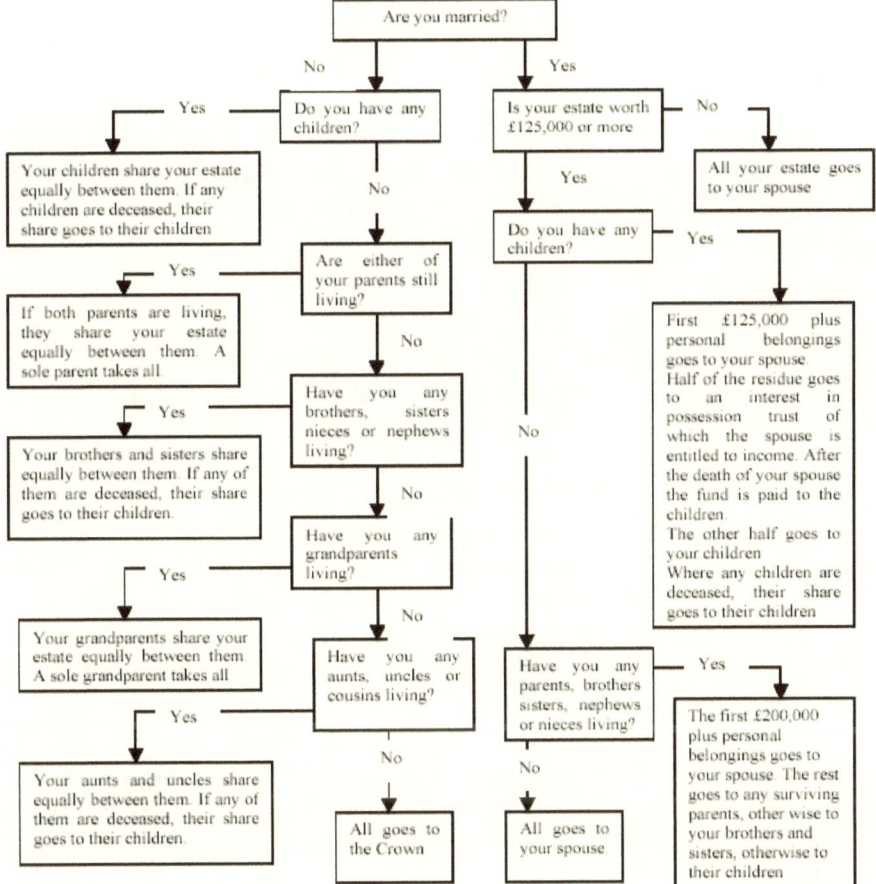

- These rules apply in English law only and are correct as of January 2005.
- Please note that this is merely a simplification of the law and not a definitive guide
- Inheritance for children under the age of eighteen is held in trust until their eighteenth birthday or until their marriage, whichever is earlier.
- Half-siblings will only benefit where there are none of the whole blood (or their children) remaining.

Example One

If you are married with children and have an estate worth more than £125,000, here's what happens. The first £125,000 only goes to your spouse. Half of the residue goes to your spouse in the form of a trust in which he or she has a lifetime interest in possession. The other half goes to the children.

Example Two

If you are married with no children but have siblings, parents, nieces, and nephews and an estate worth more than £125,000, here's what happens. The first £200,000 goes to your spouse. The rest goes to your surviving parents, brothers, nieces, nephews, aunties, uncles, and cousins.

Example Three

This is my favourite one. I like this one, and it's horrible really. Do you have any children? No. Are either of your parents alive? No. Have you any brothers, sisters, nephews, or nieces? No. Have you any grandparents? No. Have you uncles, aunties, and cousins? No. In that case, it all goes to the state so they're going to get it all anyway! That's the laws of intestacy. You can have a look. They are shown in the illustration. Most people just don't believe it. They just don't believe that's how the laws of intestacy work. Trust me. They really do. You see wills are about common sense. Wills are about dictating what it is you want to happen.

Prior to October 2007, many clients were advised to take advantage of the double nil rate band allowances by utilising a will trust arrangement within their wills. In simple language, this meant that each of the spouses completed a will, passing everything to each other with the first £300,000 going into a trust so that, on the death of the second spouse, the first £300,000 allowance was utilised. The second £300,000 allowance was available on the second death, so, effectively, £600,000 was removed from the estate for inheritance tax purposes. In his pre-budget statement in October 2007, the Chancellor removed this need to set up a double nil rate band trust.

To put it simply, there has been no doubling of the inheritance tax nil rate band. The Chancellor has only formalised an arrangement that already existed. Most clients who had taken sensible tax advice and appropriate tax planning were already utilising these allowances. For those of you who are reading this book who have utilised the nil rate bands with a will trust arrangement, which are often in conjunction with an IOU trust, these arrangements can remain in your wills as they presently are. Many of you may also have arranged to own your properties as tenants in common. This enables you to leave half the house on the first death and utilise the nil rate band as highlighted above. If you have arranged this, there is no reason to change the ownership back to joint tenants.

The effect of the new arrangements does have substantial benefit for those clients who had not utilised their double nil rate bands. This also applies to existing widows and widowers where the spouse had died prior to the new announcements being made in October 2007. All married couples and those in civil partnerships now effectively have a £600,000 nil rate band allowance. On current estimates, it seems this will cost the Inland Revenue approximately £1 billion per year. However, it still means that some £3 billion will be collected in inheritance tax. I suspect that many of you reading this book will fall into the category of clients who have estates that are valued at more than £600,000. Therefore, you will still be subject to inheritance tax.

How Much Flexibility and Control?

1. Give away Capital, Income and Growth

2. Give away Capital and Growth, keep Income

3. Give away Growth keep Capital and Income

Chapter Seven

What Are the Inheritance Tax Exemptions?

Let's take a look at the good news. There are multiple exemptions to inheritance taxes that you can utilise to save money for your heirs. This chapter provides a brief summary of them.

£3,000 Exemption

You can give away £3,000 per annum that is free of inheritance tax. Husbands can give away £3,000 to their children. Wives can give away £3,000 to their children. Please note that isn't £3,000 to each child. It's a total of £3,000. So, if you have three children, that's £1,000 each.

One lady I saw last year had actually given £3,000 each to her four children. She thought it was £3,000 each. No, it's a total of £3,000, but you do get one year's grace. So you could go back one year.

If you didn't do it for last year, you could say to me now, 'Well, could I give £3,000, John, for last year?'

I would say, 'Yes, you can.'

You could ask, 'Can I give £3,000 for this year?'

I would say, 'Yes, you can.'

You would ask, 'Can my wife do that?'

I would say, 'Yes, she can.'

So, utilising the £3,000 exemption, that's £12,000 you can give away today. And you don't have to live seven years. The day you make the gift, it's outside the estate immediately. So there's no seven-year rule applying to the annual £3,000 gifting allowance.

Small Gift Exemption

You can give away £250 to as many people as you wish. That's a very nice exemption that I use every year for my three grandchildren. Bradley is fourteen now. Nathan is ten, and Emma is eight. Now I don't actually give them the money. I'm not being mean. Some years ago, I took out a savings scheme for them when they were born.

When they are eighteen, I'll say to them, 'Here you are. Here's the money towards your first motor car, or here's some money towards your university and school fees, or, here's some money towards your first deposit on your first house.'

That money has been building up very nicely over the years. So I invest a total of £750 a year for the three grandchildren. It's just a nice way of building up some tax-free funds for them for when they get to be eighteen. They have no idea I'm doing this. As I say, I have done so for a number of years. It's lovely how it builds up, a nice, tax-free lump sum.

I also run a share portfolio for them. They do know about that. Bradley, in particular, is very keen and interested in which shares I buy and sell.

In Consideration of Marriage Exemption

You can give money in consideration of marriage: £5,000 to your children; £2,500 to your grandchildren; and £1,000 to any others. It's quite a useful way to give some money away if you have some spare cash.

Normal Expenditure Rule Exemption

Another exemption is normal expenditure out of income. Now that's a very interesting one. It might apply to a few of you reading this book. If you can justify to Inland Revenue that you've got spare income, not spare capital, you can give some of that income away in addition to all these other allowances.

So let's paint a picture. You've got income of £30,000 a year. That's made up of your pension income, investment income, and building society income. It doesn't matter where it comes from. It's just income. You can show the Inland Revenue that you've been living off £20,000 a year for the last few years because you've been saving £10,000 a year in the bank or building society. The Inland Revenue will allow you to take that £10,000 and give it to your children or grandchildren in addition to these other allowances. But it's got to come out of your income, not your capital.

I have many clients who give away out of their income. One such client gives his children £17,000 a year in addition to all these other allowances. Another client gives £30,000 a year to his daughter in addition to all the other allowances. The Inland Revenue allows all of it because it's coming out of income.

So think about this exemption. If you've got spare income and you'd like to consider giving some of it away, do so. Otherwise, it will continue to accumulate within your estate and just attract additional inheritance tax.

Potentially Exempt Transfers

Not cats and dogs, but potentially exempt transfers hinge on the seven-year rule.

You can make a gift, no matter how much. As long as you live seven years, it'll be outside of your estate. But you can't make a gift with reservation. It's why you can't give away your house.

You can't say, 'Well, here you are, darling children. Here's my house. I'll give it to you, and I'll carry on living here.'

The Inland Revenue will say, 'Well, you can do that. You can give it to your children, but you can't carry on living there unless you pay the full rent that the property would let for in the high street.'

Unless you pay your children £20,000 a year in rent, you can't claim that for inheritance tax purposes.

And it's no good for you to say to the kids that you'll give them the property and pay them a pound a year. Then you nod and wink.

The Inland Revenue will not allow that. They've tightened up enormously on these rules to make sure you can't have a gift with reservation. You either make a gift or you don't.

If I want to say to somebody, 'Here's my pen. Please take it with my compliments and keep it.'

That's absolutely fine for inheritance tax, but, the moment I tell the person that I want my pen back, as far as the Inland Revenue is concerned, I never made a gift in the first place. It's that simple. You either make a gift or you don't. If you make a gift, you have to give the income away with the gift as well. That's where the problem comes in for most of you in terms of giving away potentially exempt transfers.

But, if you have the wherewithal or some spare cash or shares and would like to give some to the children or grandchildren, please do so. I gave some to my two daughters eight years ago, so that's outside of my estate and completely free of inheritance tax. It's well worth doing, providing you're happy that you can afford to do it.

Nil Rate Band

It seems that everyone is familiar with the so-called nil rate band, which, at present, means £300,000 is taxed at 0 per cent. The Chancellor has announced this will be increased over the coming years as follows:

Tax year	Nil Rate Band
2007/08	300000

2008/09	312500
2009/10	325000
2010/11	350000

Mr Gordon Brown has been appointed to the position of Prime Minister, and Mr Alistair Darling has taken over as the new Chancellor. Suddenly, inheritance tax has become a political football. The recent announcement by the Conservatives that they would increase the nil rate band to £1 million really put the cat amongst the pigeons! As a result, in October 2007, the Labour Party announced they would allow utilisation of the double nil rate band for all married couples and civil partnerships. In simple language, all married couples and civil partnerships will automatically get £600,000 nil rate band allowance.

Obviously, this could be of great benefit to a number of people reading this book. However, always beware of chancellors making gifts. As Nigel May of Accountants MacIntyre Hudson stated in *The Daily Mail* on October 19, 2007: "The Chancellor has done some wonderful arithmetic here by adding together two allowances that already exist and passing it off as a doubling of the allowance".

In other words, most people who did any sensible tax planning with regard to inheritance tax automatically arranged their wills so they were both utilising the nil rate band. Thus, they had the benefit of £600,000 falling outside of their estates.

Only the people who didn't make wills or hadn't arranged to take advantage of the nil rate bands will benefit from the Chancellor's new rules. It is estimated that, in the tax year 2007/2008, the Chancellor will collect £3.8 billion in inheritance tax. Following these proposed changes, there will be reduction in the inheritance tax of approximately £1 billion. This still means some £2.6 billion will be collected in inheritance tax. Obviously, this will apply to anyone with an estate worth more than £600,000, which, of course, includes your home. Many of you reading this book will have arranged nil rate band discretionary trusts commonly in conjunction with an IOU. At present, a huge debate is raging within the UK as to whether it is necessary to change your wills and remove these schemes or leave them in situ. As I have to come down on one side of the fence or other to give appropriate advice, on balance, I would suggest that, if you already have these schemes within your will, you leave them as they are. They will still work and save the inheritance tax as originally planned. To put it another way, I have these arrangements myself. I have not changed them to date.

Charitable Tax Allowances

Gifts to UK-recognised charities are all free of inheritance tax. So, if you want to give everything to charity, there'll be no inheritance tax to pay. And I do actually have a lady giving £1 million to the Royal National Lifeboat Institution. All of that will be free of inheritance tax because it is a charity. Surprisingly, gifts to political parties are also free of inheritance tax!

Last year, a gentleman shouted out at one of my seminars, 'Can I form my own political party?'

So I checked the legislation. You actually can, but you have to put candidates up at a number of constituencies at the next election. So I suppose, by the time you've worked out how much that would cost you, it would be considerably more than the inheritance tax that you would save.

Remember that income is king, but you can arrange your investments to produce more income and reduce inheritance tax.

Key Questions

16. Are you saving the maximum inheritance tax?
17. Are you taking advantage of all the tax exemptions?

What Is Taxable?

The question of which assets are taxable and how you can manage your estate to avoid these taxes is our next topic. Cash, gilts, securities, property, and the other assets discussed previously are all considered part of your taxable estate when you die. By utilising the seven-year rule, using tenants in common titles, and gifting strategies, you can substantially decrease your estate tax liabilities.

The Seven-year Rule

A father came to my seminar. He heard me say that he could make a gift to his daughter. If he lived seven years, that would be outside his estate and free of inheritance tax. The same could apply to you.

'So, here you are, darling,' he could say. 'I love you so much that here's £100,000. Take it and spend it. Do what you wish with it. Of course, I never want it back. If I or your mum has to go to a nursing home and need long-term health care, well, that's just our tough luck. But it will save a lot of inheritance tax.'

With that as a background, I suppose all of you have made substantial gifts to your children, have you not? The reason for that is the same reason we've all got. How long are you going to live? How long are you going to need the money for? It's all very well giving it to the children or grandchildren to save inheritance tax. But is it giving you enough to live on for the rest of your lives? That's a really important issue. Anyway, children don't always turn out the way we think they will. In an ideal world, the sky is blue, the grass is green, the sun is shining, and the children are terrific.

'Here you are you, darlings,' you could say. 'Here's £50,000 each.'

A few years later, they say, 'It's a shame that you're going to a nursing home, Dad. But you gave us this money. We've spent it having a good old time. Thank you very much indeed.'

You have no control over that money once you've given it away. However, remember to always be nice to your children. After all, they will choose your nursing home!

Key Questions

18. What's stopping you from getting around to it?
19. How much money would you like to gift to your family?

Tenants in Common

Until four years ago, a number of schemes were available to enable clients to put their house into a trust. They could continue to live there, but they'd still have the benefit of saving inheritance tax. However, the Inland Revenue never officially approved these schemes, so the Chancellor decided to close these schemes on the pretext that, because they had never been approved, they were tax evasion and not genuine tax avoidance. This caused much anguish with many clients who had entered into various schemes, which then had to be disbanded.

But property is not a liquid asset. This makes it very difficult to dispose of it or do anything with it, especially if it is your residence. However, there is a way of changing the ownership of your house to tenants in common, which can enable you to utilise your nil rate band for inheritance tax. These days, most homes are owned jointly. In simple language, this means that, on the death of either spouse, the house simply passes to the surviving spouse without any further difficulty. By changing the ownership of the house to tenants in common, a married couple are able to arrange their affairs so the husband legally owns half of the house and the wife legally owns half of the house. In this way, on the death of the first spouse, half of the house can be left into a trust, which gives a lifetime interest in possession to the surviving spouse. But it will not go to the ultimate beneficiaries, normally the children, until the death of the surviving spouse. In his budget in 2006, the Chancellor made lots of changes with regard to these types of trusts. But it did not affect spouses, so it is still possible to take advantage of this type of arrangement.

Chapter Eight

Gift Plan

This idea involves giving away capital, income, and growth. That's a total gift. This means you've got no interest in it. The main problem is maintaining flexibility and control. So, if you set up a gift plan, it's designed to reduce your liability for tax and simplify your investments. This will only apply to a few of you reading this book. Most of you don't want to give your money away. If you do, this will work very well for you. This arrangement is suitable for the following: those with an IHT problem; single people or married couples; those without an income requirement; or those with available capital.

Here, a gift is made into an investment bond, which is subject to a trust. It's as simple as that … gift, bond, and then trust. It's very straightforward. Now, over a period of time, the money that has been invested, the gift, is inside the estate for seven years, but all the growth is outside the estate. After seven years, the total amount falls outside the estate. It is all free of inheritance tax.

Discounted Gift Plan

One scheme that will appeal to at least half of you reading this book, if you like the idea of giving away capital and growth as long as you know you have always got access to the income, is to utilise a discounted gift plan. It doesn't matter what your estate is worth. If it grows by another £100,000, it is of no material benefit.

You could say, 'But, if I can give that growth away to my children and save inheritance tax on it, that is something I'd like to do.'

That's what I am talking about here with regard to a discounted gift plan. This is how it works. It's designed to immediately reduce your liability to inheritance tax on part of the investment with the rest falling outside the estate under the seven-year rule. It is suitable for the following: those with an IHT problem; single people or married couples; those with an income requirement; or those with available capital.

How the Scheme Works

First, an investment is made into a bond. This is the same investment bond I mentioned earlier. This time, the bond goes into a trust. It is called the discounted gift trust, which is an approved trust. Inside the trust, it breaks it down into what's called your fund and the beneficiary's fund. The Inland Revenue immediately discounts your fund. The second part, the beneficiary's fund, is a potentially exempt transfer. It can be transferred under the seven-year rule. This is usually referenced as a chargeable lifetime transfer.

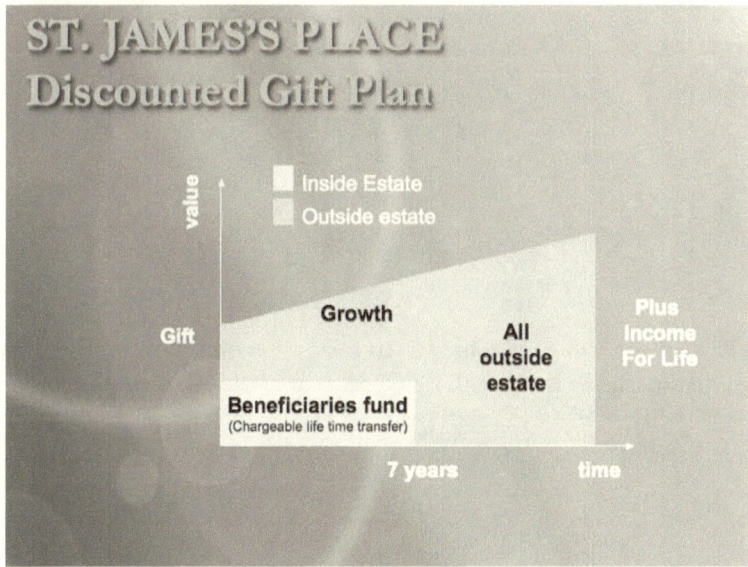

How the Scheme Comes Together

First of all, your fund is immediately discounted. This part of the investment is outside the estate and free of inheritance tax. The growth on your fund and the beneficiary's fund is outside the estate and free of inheritance tax. The beneficiary's fund, however, stays in the estate for seven years. After that point, it's now all outside the estate. But you can still carry on taking the income towards your long-term health and nursing care requirements as well as whatever other reason you'd want to take the income for. It's a very attractive scheme. I set up a lot of these schemes, and they work.

The Plan in More Detail

You invest into a bond. You take an income. We agree up front that you're going to have normally 2.5 or 5 per cent. The bond is placed in the discounted gift trust. The discount is established with the Inland Revenue. The trust fund is divided into two parts, your fund and the beneficiary's fund. The trust gives you an income for life. On death, everything goes to the beneficiaries. So let's have a look at some samples of the discounts.

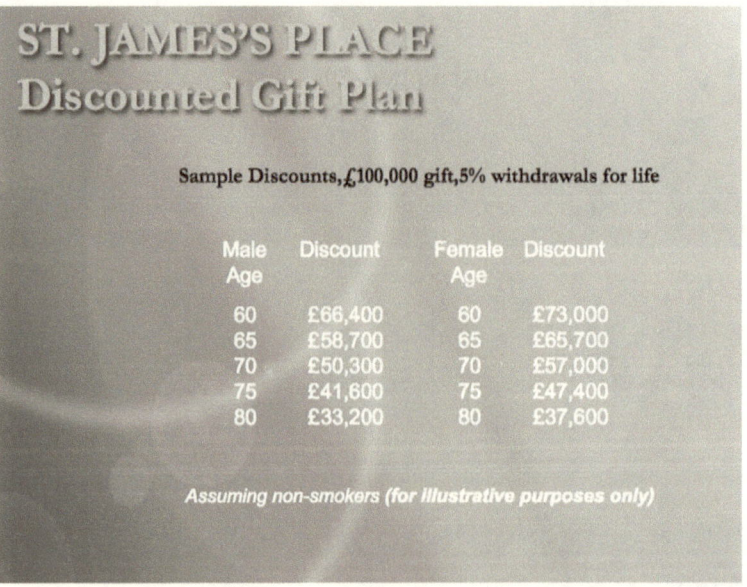

ST. JAMES'S PLACE
Discounted Gift Plan

Sample Discounts, £100,000 gift, 5% withdrawals for life

Male Age	Discount	Female Age	Discount
60	£66,400	60	£73,000
65	£58,700	65	£65,700
70	£50,300	70	£57,000
75	£41,600	75	£47,400
80	£33,200	80	£37,600

*Assuming non-smokers (for **illustrative** purposes only)*

For a sixty-year-old male, the agreed Inland Revenue discount for £100,000 going into the scheme is £66,000. So 66 per cent of the investment is outside the estate immediately. If you're a sixty-year-old female, then it's 73 per cent. You get a bigger discount for a female because you're going to live longer.

If you are male, sixty years old, and put £1 million in, that means £660,000 is outside the estate immediately. If you are female, sixty years old, and put £1 million in, that means £730,000 is outside your estate immediately.

Gift and Loan Plan

This plan is very popular. Let's have a look at it. It is designed to reduce your liability, provide you with an income, and simplify your investments. It is suitable for the following: those with IHT problem; single people or couples; those with an income requirement; those without an income requirement; or those with available capital.

How It Works

You make a gift into a bond. This is that same bond I keep talking about. This time, it goes into a gift and loan trust. There, we split it into a gift bond and a loan bond. Let's have a look to see what happens here.

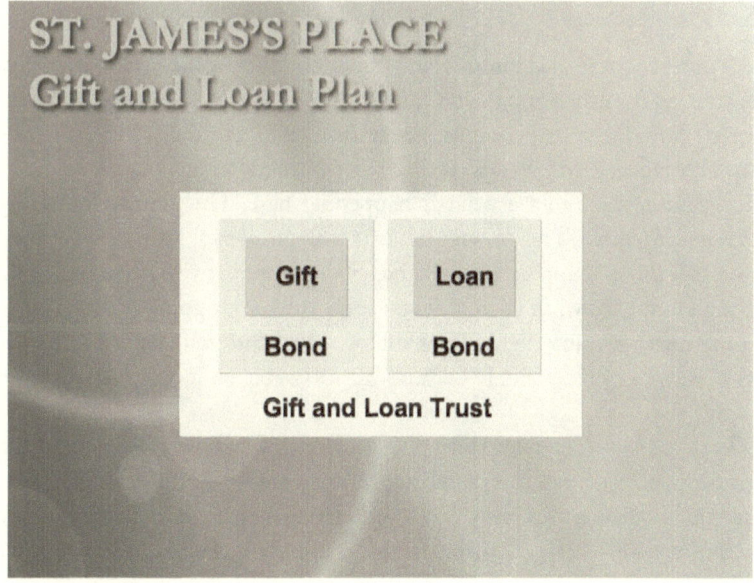

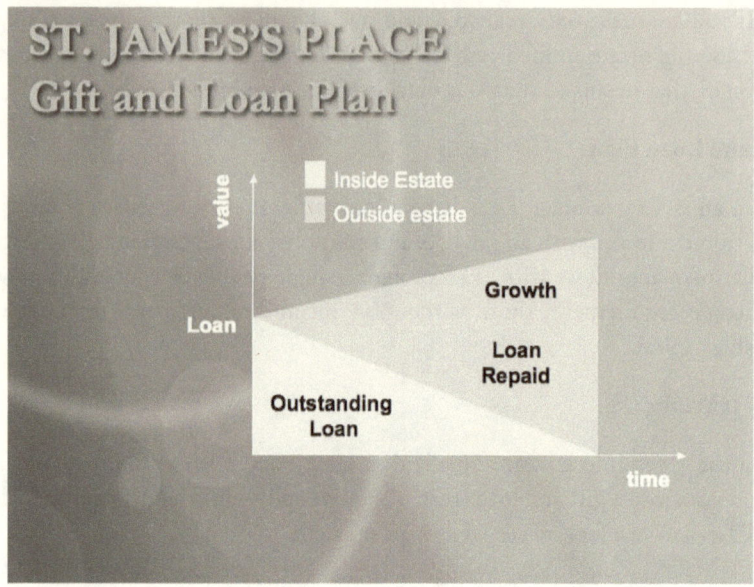

An investment is made into an investment bond. On the face of it, it all stays inside your estate, even though you can see all of the growth is outside the estate. But here's how the scheme works. Every time you take the 5 per cent tax-free income allowance, it will go against the outstanding loan on your estate. So, from the illustration, you can see what is happening here. The amount outside your estate is getting more. The amount that's taxable inside your estate is getting less. I always call this a 'dripping tap scheme.' For example, if you go to bed at night, you put an empty bowl in your sink and leave the tap dripping. When you come down the next morning, the bowl is full of water. But you and I know it didn't fill with water immediately. It became full of water as it gradually dripped in overnight.

That's the way the gift and loan plan works. It's a gradual scheme. It's dripping in, drip, drip, drip, drip. But it's amazing how it grows over the years. I have some clients who I saw very recently. They've been clients of mine for about twenty years. But, twelve years ago, these particular clients invested £200,000. It's now worth over £600,000. It's in a gift and loan scheme, which means we now have £400,000 outside the estate, completely free of inheritance tax.

Unfortunately, I get many cases where I meet the beneficiaries whose parents didn't do this. It's your choice always as to whether you save the tax or not. I'm not saying that you must save inheritance tax. I'm not saying that at all. It's entirely up to you. But, if you do want to save it, then these are legitimate schemes to enable you to do that.

In summary, you set up a trust and lend the balance of available capital to the trust. The trust lends the capital to be invested into an investment bond. I will do all this for you. You just tell me how much you want to invest, and I will do the rest.

I always say to my clients, 'When you drive a car, do you need to know exactly how the engine works?'

Most clients will respond, 'Not really.'

In order to drive the car, you need to know it will take you from A to B. You don't need to know exactly how the engine functions. This is a point with regard to inheritance tax plans and the gift and loan scheme. It is really quite a simple plan to those of us who have been involved in setting them up for thirty-five years, but it is not so easy to get your brain around when you haven't come into contact with it before.

In essence, I am saying, 'Trust me. I'm a financial adviser. I will give you the best advice.'

Fund Your Liability (Life Assurance)

This approaches the problem from a different angle. You can utilise your income or your capital on this one, but it's utilising something different, a life assurance policy. It isn't an ordinary life insurance. It's a special type called joint life second death because we know when this problem is going to apply to you. It won't apply when you or your spouse dies. It's when the second of you dies. Let's have a look to see how this might work because there is a slight difference on this one with regard to the other schemes I have talked about so far. It is suitable for the following: those with IHT problems; single people or married couples; those with available income; those with available capital; or those who are insurable for life assurance.

This type of scheme utilises a life assurance policy, so please don't ask your adviser to do this after your health has deteriorated. He or she can't.

Life Insurance

Let's have a look at this to see how it might work. Quite a number of you reading this book would qualify for life insurance. It's amazing how many people do these days. People in their seventies and eighties do qualify for life insurance, but, of course, you've got to be fit for your age and be able to afford the premium.

The idea of utilising the life insurance is to set up a guaranteed trust fund so, on the day you die, money comes in to meet the tax liability. It's in a trust that's outside your estate, so your beneficiaries can use it to get probate granted immediately because they use it to pay off the Inland Revenue.

So you have an estate worth £800,000, and the tax liability is £80,000. You'll put £80,000 into that guaranteed trust fund, so, on the day you die, £80,000 is paid off. That's the end of the problem. Very simple and straightforward.

You might ask how are you going to pay for it.

Well, you could pay for it out of your income, or you could pay for it out of your capital.

Let's have a look at how you might pay for it utilising your income.

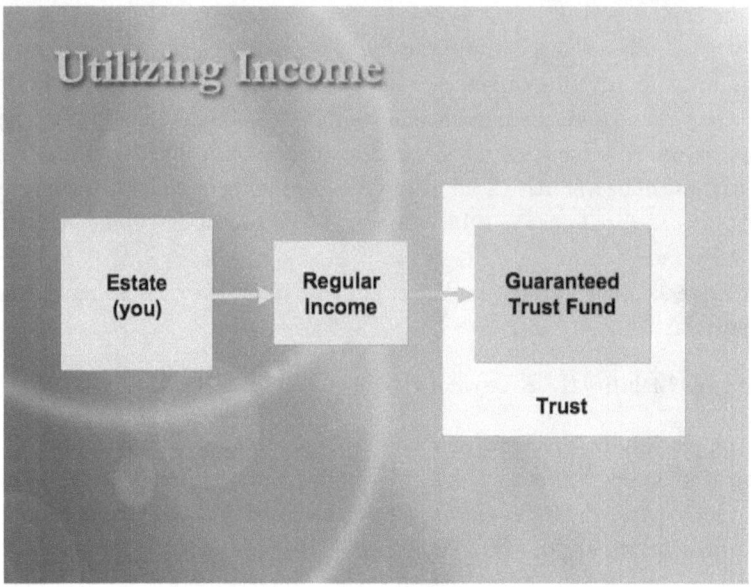

Paying for It from Your Income

If you pay out of your regular income, where would your income come from? The answer would be from your pension, investments, bank, or building society. It doesn't matter where it comes from. You just take that income to pay the premium on a life insurance to give you the guaranteed trust fund. It's as simple as that. Very straightforward.

You might say, 'Ah, well, that's all right, John. But I haven't really got enough income. I can't really afford the premium on this.'

I could say, 'Well, okay. Let's look at your capital then. Your capital's created the problem. Let's see if we can use your capital to help solve the problem. Let's take some of your money and make a gift of it. Let's get it into one of those investment bonds, that bond we keep talking about. From that bond, let's take some income into the guaranteed trust by utilising the 5 per cent tax-free allowance to pay the premium for the guaranteed trust fund.'

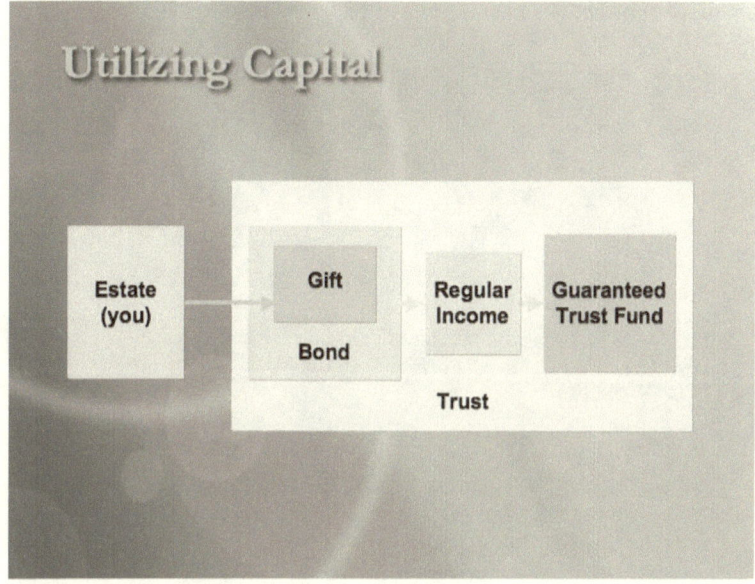

That's a very attractive way of doing it. The premium for the insurance, of course, will depend very much on your ages. Here are some examples. Please note that it's guaranteed.

The Sum Assured Is Guaranteed the Day You Pay the Premium

From the table, if you're a sixty-five-year-old male married to a sixty-year-old female and you need £100,000 inheritance tax protection utilising a life assurance policy, the premium will be £2,400 per annum, that is, 2.4 per cent. If you are a seventy-year-old male married to a sixty-five-year-old female, the premium would be £3,000 per annum, that is, 3 per cent. A seventy-five-year-old male married to a seventy-year-old female would find that the premium would be £3,800 per annum, that is, 3.8 per cent on £100,000 sum assured. The life assurance policy is a very simple vehicle in reality. You pay the premium. The insurance actuary calculates the rates. When the second of you dies, they pay out the appropriate sum assured.

On average, most clients can never pay in what the insurance company will pay out one day. If you look at the table for a sixty-five-year-old male married to a sixty-year-old female, you will see that you have to live about forty-five years before you can pay in what the insurance company is guaranteed to pay out one day, that is, the £100,000.

You may ask, 'How can the insurance company make a profit on this deal?' The answer is very simple. They win on some cases and lose on others. But they make an actuarial calculation as to how long they will have the use of your money, which they invest and live off the interest over the appropriate number of years. A life assurance contract is a magic piece of paper as it creates capital where capital did not exist before.

Cost of a Guaranteed Trust Fund assuming Inheritance Tax Liability of £100,000		
Male 65 Female 60	2.4%	£2,400 per annum
Male 70 Female 65	3.0%	£3,000 per annum
Male 75 Female 70	3.8%	£3,800 per annum

Assuming Non Smokers **(for illustrative purposes only)**

With insurance, you're just playing with the odds. We all know that every single person reading this book knows that he or she is going to die. All of us hope it's a long time in the future, but the reality is that's going to happen. So that's what the life insurance contract is. It's based on the actuarial calculation of how long you're going to live and how long the average person will live to produce the level of premium. It's very attractive in the right circumstances, provided you are insurable. But you do have to be insurable.

Key Question

20. What life insurance do you have?

Summary of Options

(1) Utilise your allowances on death utilising the nil rate band.
(2) Give your assets away whilst you are alive.
(3) Fund for your liability.
(4) Put together a combination of the above.

I understand that a lot of you do believe you are immortal. The ones who don't probably take the following view, 'In view of my firm belief in reincarnation, I do hereby direct that my entire estate be held in trust pending my return to this earth.'

So, if you think you're going to come back again, why not leave it in a tin box and pick it up on the way back in? It would be nice if you could do that, wouldn't it? But remember that you can't take it with you.

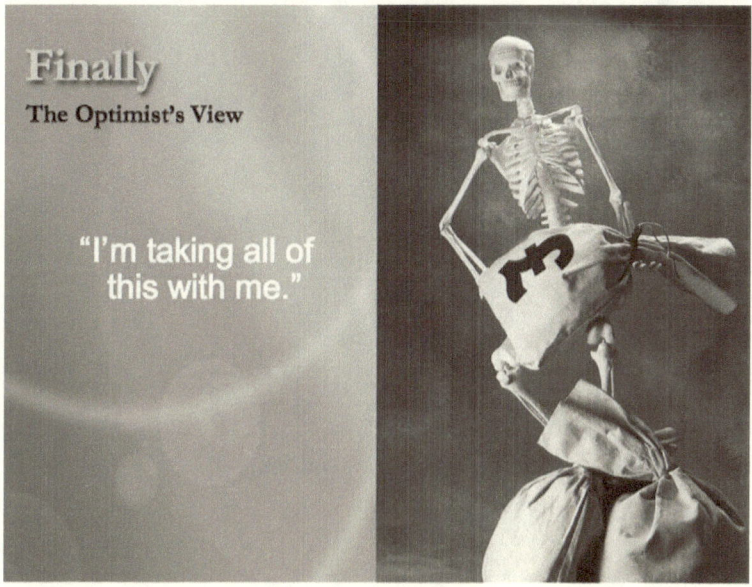

Finally
The Optimist's View

"I'm taking all of this with me."

The Next Step

The next step is to meet with a financial adviser such as myself. The meeting is confidential. You would fill in a questionnaire form, similar to the one at the back of this book, either prior to the meeting and send it to him or her or have it available at the meeting. The financial adviser will review your current situation and look to see what can be done to help you. You are under no obligation at all. These visits are free, and they are in your home. So you have everything to gain and nothing to lose. Hopefully, as you have seen by reading this book, much can be done to help you both with regard to your investments to help you enrich your retirement as well as substantially reduce your inheritance tax liability.

'He talked a lot of sense. It's a lot of food for thought, especially on the inheritance side.'

Mr and Mrs Price, Woodbridge

'I found it very, very interesting.'

Mr Newman, Haverhill

'His presentation is absolutely excellent.'

Mrs Chamberlain, Ipswich

'I thought it was very interesting.'

Mr Michaels, Northampton

'Excellent presentation.'

Mr Shah, London

'Very good; very interesting. Makes you be able to focus on all the problems that we're probably going to leave behind.'

Mr Gentle, Long Melford

'I found it's a lot of information that I didn't know that has changed from years before that I didn't really understand. But it's made it very clear.'

Mr Reed, Cambridge

'He works without notes, which is astonishing. He thoroughly knows his subjects. It's all a bit too quick, of course, to make any lasting impressions. I don't remember anything, but I've written down quite useful things. It needs a meeting obviously to discuss the personal arrangements.'

Mrs Noble, London

'Very good speaker.'

Mr Walker, Ascot

'Very clear. And in simple terms that we can understand, which, of course, is what people want really. Plain, simple talking so you personally can understand it.

Mr and Mrs Williams, Sudbury

'I thought it was very clear and quite frightening some of it. I hadn't actually realised how low the bank interest rates were, although I knew they were going down. That's made me decide to move some of my money. I was interested in hearing the inheritance tax plans that are available to people, and I shall be certainly looking at that.'

Mr Smith, Hintlesham

'I thought John was very, very informative. That's my first visit. I do not have any money with you, but I might in the future. I thought he was exceedingly well–informed. Knows his subject totally. I'm totally unbiased. I've never seen this company before, but I am impressed.'

Mr Johnson, Oakham

ST. JAMES'S PLACE
PARTNERSHIP

CONFIDENTIAL
CLIENT QUESTIONNAIRE

Client 1 Name:	
Client 2 Name:	
Advisors Name:	John Cross/Chris Cooke - www.sjpp.co.uk/johncross
Seminar attended:	
Date of seminar:	
Date of meeting(s):	— —
Date Initial Disclosure Document given to Client:	
Date Menu given to Client:	

PERSONAL AND FAMILY DETAILS

CONTACT DETAILS

	Client 1	Client 2
Full Name & Title		
Home Address		
	Postcode	Postcode
Telephone No		Email Address:

PERSONAL DETAILS

	Client 1		Client 2	
Date of Birth/Age		Age		Age
Marital Status				
	Smoker	Non Smoker	Smoker	Non Smoker

CHILDREN & OTHER DEPENDANTS

Name	Age	Sex M/F	Marital Status	Relationship to client Client 1	Client 2	Dependant Y/N	Until When

OCCUPATION AND EARNINGS

OCCUPATION

	Client 1	Client 2
Occupation/Retired		

GROSS ANNUAL INCOME £

	Client 1	Client 2	Joint
Income from employment			
Self-employed income			
State Pension Income			
Pension Income			
Investment Income			
Rental Income			
Income from other sources			
Total Gross Annual Income (before tax)			

MONTHLY EXPENDITURE

	Client 1	Client 2	Joint
Total Net Monthly Income (after tax) (A)	£	£	£
Total Monthly Expenditure (B)	£	£	£
Disposable Net Income (A-B)	£	£	£

ASSETS £

	Owned by Client 1 Amount in £	Owned by Client 2 Amount in £	Owned Jointly Amount in £
Main Residence			
Other Property			
Cash/Building Society Deposits			
TOISAs			
National Savings/ Gilts			
PEP's & ISA's			
Unit Trusts & OEICs			
Investment Bonds			
Stocks & Shares			
Personal Assets			
Life plans not in trust			
Value of trust property in which you have an interest in possession			
Monies owing to you			
Other Assets			
Total Assets			

LIABILITIES £

	Owed by Client 1 Amount in £	Owed by Client 2 Amount in £	Owed Jointly Amount in £
Mortgages			
Loans and Credit Cards			
Other (eg secured/guaranteed)			
Total Liabilities			

SUMMARY OF ASSETS AND LIABILITIES £

	Client 1	Client 2	Joint
Assets less Liabilities	A	B	C
Total estate for IHT purposes (A+B+C)			

TAX AND RESIDENCE

PERSONAL TAX / RESIDENCE / DOMICILE STATUS

	Client 1				Client 2			
Are you chargeable to UK tax?	Yes	No	Highest Rate	%	Yes	No	Highest Rate	%
Are you currently resident in the UK for tax purposes?	Yes	No			Yes	No		
Are you domiciled in the UK for tax purposes?	Yes	No			Yes	No		
If non-domiciled, when did you first arrive in the UK?								

YOUR PRIORITIES

What is important to you? (please tick as appropriate)

	Very Important		Fairly Important		Not a Priority	
	Client 1	Client 2	Client 1	Client 2	Client 1	Client 2
Investing for Growth	☐	☐	☐	☐	☐	☐
Investing for Income	☐	☐	☐	☐	☐	☐
Investing for Income & Growth	☐	☐	☐	☐	☐	☐
To create capital for future use	☐	☐	☐	☐	☐	☐
Reducing Inheritance Tax	☐	☐	☐	☐	☐	☐
Creating a fund to pay a potential Inheritance Tax liability	☐	☐	☐	☐	☐	☐

Please read the enclosed 'Guide to choosing your attitude to risk' before completing this section

ATTITUDE TO RISK FOR INVESTMENT PLANNING (please tick as appropriate)

Risk Categories		Low		Low to Medium		Medium		Medium to High		High	
Client 1	1		2		3		4		5		
Client 2	1		2		3		4		5		

EMERGENCY FUNDS

	Client 1	Client 2	Joint
Do you have immediate access to an emergency fund?	Yes ☐ No ☐	Yes ☐ No ☐	Yes ☐ No ☐
If yes, please detail amount	£	£	£
Do you need additional Emergency Funds?	Yes ☐ No ☐	Yes ☐ No ☐	Yes ☐ No ☐
If yes, please detail amount	£	£	£

ISA & CAPITAL GAINS TAX (CGT) ALLOWANCES

	Client 1	Client 2
Have you invested into an ISA this tax year?	Yes ☐ No ☐	Yes ☐ No ☐
If yes, give details of type – Mini/Maxi? Cash/Stocks & Shares?	£	£
Do you regularly use your CGT Allowance?	Yes ☐ No ☐	Yes ☐ No ☐
Have you used, or do you intend to use, your CGT allowance for this tax year?	Yes ☐ No ☐	Yes ☐ No ☐

Any other relevant information:

WILL ARRANGEMENTS

Client 1

Have you made a will? Yes ☐ No ☐

Date of last review _____

Is the nil rate band being used for Inheritance Tax Planning? Yes ☐ No ☐

Details of Beneficiaries (including charities)	Details (financial amounts/%)

Client 2

Have you made a will? Yes ☐ No ☐

Date of last review _____

Is the nil rate band being used for Inheritance Tax Planning? Yes ☐ No ☐

Details of Beneficiaries (including charities)	Details (financial amounts/%)

GIFTS YOU INTEND TO MAKE

Who will be making the gift? (please delete as applicable)	Value of gift (£)	Intended beneficiary(ies)	When do you intend to make the gift?
Client 1/Client 2/Joint			
Client 1/Client 2/Joint			
Client 1/Client 2/Joint			

DETAILS OF GIFTS MADE IN THE LAST 14 YEARS

Who made the gift? (please delete as applicable)	Value of gift (£)	Names of beneficiary(ies)	Date gift was made	Was the gift made into a trust?	Purpose eg Education fees for grandchild
Client 1/Client 2/Joint					
Client 1/Client 2/Joint					
Client 1/Client 2/Joint					

INHERITANCES

	Client 1	Client 2
Have you received an inheritance in the last two years?	Yes ☐ No ☐	Yes ☐ No ☐
If **yes**, how much?	£	£

ANTICIPATED INHERITANCES

	Client 1	Client 2
Do you expect to receive an inheritance?	Yes ☐ No ☐	Yes ☐ No ☐
If **yes**, how much?	£	£

SUMMARY OF ANY PLANS THAT CAN BE USED TO ADDRESS IHT NEEDS

	Client 1	Client 2	Joint
Life assurance plans available to address IHT on death	£	£	£

Any other relevant information:

5

83

ANY OTHER RELEVANT INFORMATION

Please use the space provided below to list any other relevant information:

DECLARATION

	Client 1		Client 2	
Do you expect your financial circumstances to change in the foreseeable future?	Yes ☐	No ☐	Yes ☐	No ☐

If yes, please provide details in the space provided below.

I confirm that the information contained in this document is accurate and I understand that if I declined to answer certain questions or did not provide all relevant information then the subsequent advice given will be based on the information provided.

Client 1 Name

Signature   Date

Client 2 Name

Signature   Date

Date CFR completed

THE SERVICES WE PROVIDE

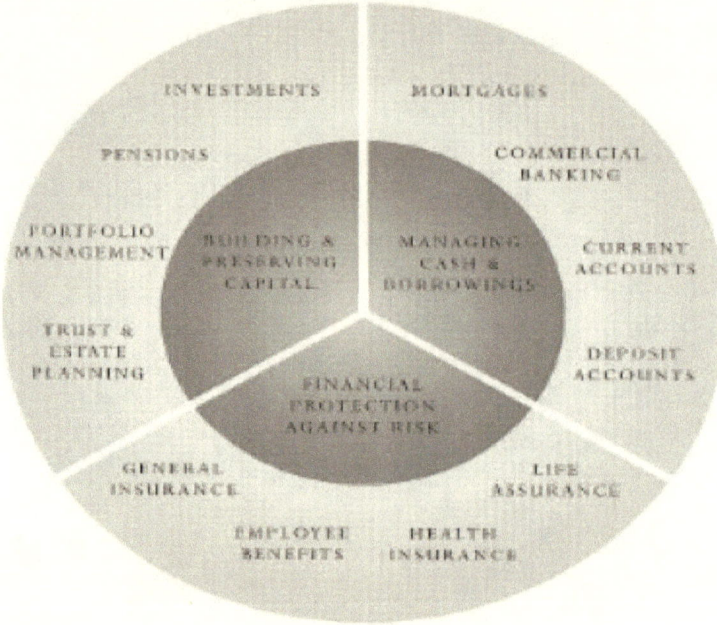

If you would like to discuss any of the other services noted above, please indicate the services that are of interest to you in the space provided on page 6.

The St. James's Place Group stands behind and guarantees the advice given by members of the St. James's Place Partnership when recommending any of the products or services provided by companies within the St. James's Place Group.

The St. James's Place Group provides investment management, risk management and selling products and services.
Members of the St. James's Place Group are authorised and regulated by the Financial Services Authority.
The St. James's Place Partnership and the title 'Partner' are the marketing terms used to describe the representatives of the St. James's Place Group.

St. James's Place plc: Registered Office St. James's Place House, Dollar Street, Cirencester, Gloucestershire, GL7 2AQ, United Kingdom.
Registered in England Number 2628062   SJP03310APR/10099

Bank

Establishment authorized by a government to accept deposits, pay interest, clear checks, make loans, act as an intermediary in financial transactions, and provide other financial services to its customers.

Beneficiary

The people to whom you leave gifts or legacies in your will or under trust.

Building Society

A form of mutual organisation owned by its depositors and borrowers. Their original purpose was to take deposits and recycle these as mortgage loans for buying houses. However, modern large building societies have extended their role such that they are now virtually the same as banks.

Capital

Measure of the accumulated financial strength of an individual, firm, or nation, created by sacrificing present consumption in favor of investment to generate future returns above investment costs.

Capital appreciation

Profit made on an investment or purchase of an asset, measured by the increase in its market value over the invested amount or cost price. Also called capital growth.

Capital Bond

A National Savings five-year bond with benefit paid in five years time. Tax is payable, however, on a yearly basis in advance.

Capital Gains Tax

Tax payable on profit made on the sale (disposal) of a capital asset, assessed and levied differently from tax on profit (income tax) realized from sale of goods or services in the normal course of a business. Often, profits on capital assets held for twelve months or longer are taxed at a favorable (lower) rate.

Capital Taxes Office

The department within HMRC responsible for collecting inheritance tax.

Chargeable Lifetime Transfer

Gifts that are immediately liable to inheritance tax at the lifetime rate.

Charitable Tax Allowance

Any funds left to charity on death are free of inheritance tax. At present, there is no upper limit.

Deed of Variation

A means of changing who benefits from someone else's estate after his or her death.

Deflation

Downturn in an economic cycle caused by circumstances or brought about by government policies. Deflation is opposite of inflation and is characterized by (1) increase in citizens' purchasing power due to the falling prices, (2) decrease in wages or slowdown in their increase due to falling levels of employment, (3) decrease in availability of credit due to higher interest rates and/or restricted money supply, and (4) decrease in imports due to lack of demand. Governments usually cause deflation to improve their balance of payments position and/or to prevent overheating of the economy by an accelerating rate of inflation. Deflation is caused either by increasing taxes and/or interest rates or by cutting down on government spending. Although effects of deflation are opposite to that of inflation, certain costs (such as minimum pay) generally do not fall. And, whereas inflation may or may not result in higher levels of output and employment, significant deflation always results in lower output and employment. See also disinflation.

Dividend

Share of the after-tax profit of a firm, distributed to its stockholders (shareholders) according to the number and class of stock (shares) held by them. Smaller firms usually distribute dividend at the end of an accounting year, whereas larger, publicly held firms usually distribute it every quarter. The amount and timing of the dividend is decided by the board of directors, who also determine whether it is paid out of current earnings or the past earnings kept as reserve. Holders of preferred stock (preference shares) receive dividend at a fixed rate and are paid first. Holders of common stock (ordinary shares) are entitled to receive any amount of dividend, based on the level of profit and the firm's need for cash for expansion or other purposes. Corporate legislation generally forbids payment of dividend out of anticipated, but not yet received (unrealized), profit. Normally all dividend payments are taxable, often at the source (the firm).

Equity

General: (1) Fairness and impartiality towards all concerned, based on the principles of evenhanded dealing. It implies giving as much advantage, consideration, or latitude to one party as it is given to another. Along with economy, effectiveness, and efficiency, equity is essential for ensuring that extent and costs of funds, goods, and services are fairly divided among their recipients. See also equitable. (2) Any right to an asset or property held by a creditor, proprietor, or stockholder (shareholder).

Accounting: (1) Ownership interest or claim of a holder of common stock (ordinary shares) and some types of preferred stock (preference shares) of a firm. On a balance sheet, equity represents funds contributed by the owners (stockholders) plus retained earnings or minus the accumulated losses. (2) Net worth of a person or firm computed by subtracting total liabilities from the total assets. In case of cooperatives, equity represents members' investment plus retained earnings or minus losses.

Equities

Common stocks (ordinary shares) traded in a securities market.

Equity ISA

If you invest in a stocks and shares ISA, you can also hold a separate cash ISA at the same time, although the total that can be invested in one year is £7,200. While you can only put £7,200 a year in an ISA, the entire balance of the ISA (i.e., the accumulated savings of several years) can be transferred into another ISA if needed, allowing you to move your ISA investments to get the best returns. Investors in equity ISAs can gain access to shares in more than forty stock exchanges across the globe, money market funds, insurance products, shares OEICs, investment trusts, unit trusts, corporate bonds and gilts, and even real estate investment trusts (REITs).

Estate

Total of all assets a person possesses and/or is beneficially entitled to. Taxable entity that comes into existence after the death of a taxpayer includes all of his or her assets (property and personal effects) and remains in existence until the assets are distributed to his or her heirs, beneficiaries, and/or claimants.

Exemption

Freedom from an obligation, restriction, or responsibility. It is also the amount that can be legally deducted from a gross income to arrive at the taxable income. See also exclusion.

FTSE 100

Financial times share index made up of 100 largest (according to market capitalization) UK firms listed on London Stock Exchange and forms the basis of futures and options traded on the London International Financial Futures Exchange (LIFFE). Popularly called 'Footsie.'

General Extension Rate

The rate that the National Savings offers on certificates that have matured beyond their normal maturity period if the investment is not surrendered.

Gift with Reservation

Gifts made to another but from which you continue to benefit. These are treated as part of your estate on death.

Gilt

Long-term fixed income debt security (bond) issued by the UK government and traded on the London Stock Exchange (or LSE, now called the International Stock Exchange of the United Kingdom and Republic of Ireland or ISE). Its name comes from the past practice of gilding the edges of a security's pages. See also treasuries.

Gross

Aggregate amount prior to any deduction or discount.

Guaranteed Income Bond

This is usually referred to as the Pensioners Bond and is now available on a one-year basis, two-year basis, and five-year basis on property prices. This refers to the value of properties, which, like all investments, can increase or decrease depending upon market circumstances. Generally speaking, property prices tend to increase with inflation and, in recent times, have been increasing ahead of inflation.

Inflation

Sustained, rapid increase in the general price level, as measured by some broad index number of prices (such as Consumer Price Index) over months or years and mirrored in the correspondingly decreasing purchasing power of the currency. It has its worst effect on the fixed-wage earners and is a disincentive to save. Any price increase alone (such as due to a crop failure), however, is not inflation. It is because such increases are self-limiting in their effect unless they cause an inflationary spiral in combination with factors such as wage increases, easier credit, or greater money supply. It is also because economies in general show some increases in prices as they recover from a recession. There is no one single, universally accepted cause of inflation, and the modern economic theory describes three types of inflation: (1) cost-push inflation due to wage increases that cause businesses to raise prices to cover higher labor costs, which leads to demand for still higher wages (the wage-price spiral), (2) demand-pull inflation resulting from increasing consumer demand financed by easier availability of credit; (3) monetary inflation caused by the expansion in money supply (due to printing of more money by a government to cover its deficits).

Inheritance Tax/IHT

Levy payable by the individual inheritor(s) of wealth (assets) received after the death of the original owner. It is usually computed inversely according to the nearness of the familial relationship of the heir to the deceased. The closer the relationship, the higher the tax. Inheritance tax is generally covered under 'capital transfer taxes,' and one of its objectives is a greater distribution of wealth in a society.

Intestate

Dying without a will. Your assets will be allocated to your spouse and/or relatives in a certain order under the intestacy rules. Different rules apply in Scotland and Northern Ireland.

ISA

A type of savings or investment account that is exempt from income and capital gains tax. You can use it to save cash or to invest in stocks and shares.

Joint Tenants

When several owners hold an asset under a joint tenancy. When one dies, the proportion of the asset he or she owned passes automatically to the surviving owners.

Managed Investment Bond

A widespread defensive investment where a fund manager will spread the investment into the main market areas such as equity, property, gilts and deposits. Different fund managers spread the investment into different percentages in different markets depending upon their views which is the best market to be in at any particular moment in time.

Market

Actual or conceptual (see marketspace) place in commercial world where forces of demand and supply operate and where buyers and sellers interact (directly or through intermediaries) to trade goods, services, or contracts or instruments for money or barter. Markets include mechanisms or means for (1) determining price of the traded item, (2) communicating the price information, (3) facilitating deals and transactions, and (4) effecting distribution. Market for a particular item is made up of existing and potential customers who need it and have the ability and willingness to pay for it. All markets, ultimately, consist of people. Also called marketplace.

Mortgage

Conveyance of the conditional right of ownership (lien) on an asset or property by its owner (the mortgagor) to a lender (the mortgagee) as security for a loan. The lien (also called lender's security interest) is recorded in the register of title documents to make it public information and is voided when the loan is repaid in full. Virtually any legally owned property can be mortgaged, although real property (land and buildings) are the most common. When personal property (appliances, cars, jewelry, etc.) is mortgaged, it is called chattel mortgage. In case of equipment, real property, and vehicles, the right of possession and use of the mortgaged item normally remains with the mortgagor, but, unless specifically prohibited in the mortgage agreement, the mortgagee has the right to take its possession (by following the prescribed procedure) at any time to protect his or her security interest. In practice, however, the courts generally do not automatically enforce this right when it involves a dwelling house and restrict it to a few specific situations. In the event of a default, the mortgagee can appoint a receiver to manage the property (if it is a business property) or obtain a foreclosure order from a court to take possession and sell it. To be legally enforceable, the mortgage must be for a definite period, and the mortgagor must have the right of redemption on payment of the debt on or before the end of that period. Mortgages are the most common type of debt instruments for several reasons such as lower rate of interest (because the loan is secured), straight forward and standard procedures, and a reasonably long repayment period. The document (debt instrument) by which this arrangement is effected is called a mortgage bill of sale or just a mortgage.

National Savings Certificates

Issued by the UK government's National Savings department. These certificates are held for one year, two years, or five years by an investor before being redeemed. No interest is paid over the five years. On redemption, all the proceeds are free of tax. If the certificates are redeemed early, the proceeds are tax-free, but the effective interest rate achieved is fairly low. If the certificates are not redeemed after five years, they continue to accrue tax-free interest but again at a fairly low rate of interest (referred to as the general extension rate).

National Savings Income Bond

An investment that pays out monthly interest. No notice or penalty for withdrawals.

Net

Amount remaining after all deductions from or adjustments to a gross figure have been made.

Nil Rate Band

The amount of the estate on which there is no inheritance tax to pay. If the estate, including any assets held in trust and gifts made within seven years of death, is less than the nil rate band, no inheritance tax will be due on it.

PEP

Tax subsidy to encourage investment in European Union company shares and UK company bonds. An investor may set up a mainstream PEP and invest £6,000 in the PEP each year. Any income or capital gains generated within the PEP is tax-free. If the PEP invests directly into shares and bonds, it must invest in shares listed on a European Stock Exchange or in a UK company's listed bonds. If the PEP invests in unit trusts or investment trusts, those funds must invest at least 50 per cent of their funds in such qualifying securities. In addition to the mainstream PEP, an individual may set up a single company PEP in which he or she may invest up to £3,000 a year. A single company PEP is only permitted to invest in the shares of one company. Since tax year 2008, all PEPs are now referred to as ISAs

Pension

Periodical or lump sum income received as a retirement benefit.

Potentially Exempt Transfer

A gift made by you during your lifetime that will not be liable to inheritance tax as long as you survive for seven years after the gift was made.

Premium bond

Bond with interest rate higher than the market interest rate and, therefore, selling at a price above its par value.

Probate

Certificate issued by a court that the will of a deceased is legally valid and that the executors appointed under the will are authorized to administer his or her estate.

Profit

Best known measure of the success of an enterprise. It is the surplus remaining after total costs are deducted from total revenue and the basis on which tax is computed and dividend is paid. Profit is reflected in reduction in liabilities, increase in assets, and/or increase in owners' equity. It furnishes resources for investing in future operations, and its absence may result in the extinction of the firm. As an indicator of comparative performance, however, it is less valuable than return on investment (ROI). In economics, total costs must include a cost to cover the normal profit for the firm. Also called earnings, gain, or income.

Property

Quality or thing owned or possessed.

Law: Article, item, or thing owned with the rights of possession, use, and enjoyment. The owner can bestow, collateralize, encumber, mortgage, sell, or transfer and can exclude everyone else from it. Two basic kinds of property are (1) real (land), involving a degree of geographical fixity, and (2) personal (anything other than real property), which does not involve geographical fixity. Personal property is subdivided into tangible property (any physical animate or inanimate object) and intangible property (intellectual property).

Retirement

Removal of an asset, equipment, property, or resource from service after its useful life or following its sale.

Share exchange

Business combination in which two firms retain their independent existence and each firm exchanges some or all of its shares with those of the other.

Share index

Alternative term for stock index. Share index is in the banking, commerce and finance, investing and securities and futures trading subjects.

Stock market

Alternative term for stock exchange. Stock market is in the accounting and auditing, banking, commerce and finance, investing and securities and futures trading subjects.

Tenants in common

Joint ownership of property where each joint tenant owns a separate share in the property. On the death of one of the joint owners, their share passes to their beneficiaries by their will or intestacy. Equity ISAs (or stocks and shares ISAs) are a way of investing up to £7,200 a year in the markets without being charged income tax or capital gains tax on profits.

Trust

A structure created by the formal transfer of assets to a small group of people (trustees) or professional trust company, which holds the assets for the benefit of others (beneficiaries).

Trustees

The legal owner of the assets within a trust that they are holding on behalf of the beneficiaries.

Volatility

Economics: Rate of change in price over a given period. Expressed often as a percentage, it is computed as the annualized standard deviation of the percentage change in the daily price.

Securities trading: Size and frequency of rapid changes in the price of a security. If the causes of volatility are peculiar to security, it is measured by alpha; if the causes are related to the securities market as a whole, it is measured by beta.

Index